The Bug Out Gardening Guide

Ron Foster

Alabama, USA

© 2014 by Ron Foster
All rights reserved.

ISBN-13: 978-1505284454
ISBN-10: 1505284457

Printed in the United States of America

Preface

What exactly is Bug Out Gardening and what sort of desperate fool would ever need to try and attempt it? You might say it is my simplified practical version of a survival manual for homesteading the Apocalypse, growing a garden when it really counts. Having your own garden in your own back yard is all well and good but what if you must actually have to evacuate and go to a remote location or start up an income augmenting garden on a bunch of bad or nutrient deficient soil without access to money or modern agricultural methods and supplies?

Most of my fellow Preppers are already realizing that besides having long term dehydrated and dried foods stored for a disaster, that one must also consider having the ability to grow replenishable fresh grown foods for supplementing their diets.

This book will teach you how simple it can be to take a garden with you when you bug out, or take along the materials you will need to create a small successful survival garden.

The idea is for you to be better than just being basically prepared, be ready to produce and be productive! Learn about growing vegetables from scratch when it absolutely matters and times are hard. Know what to do when you find the stores are all closed and lack basic the materials or resources to nurture your plants to harvest. It seems to me that far too many people are pretty flippant

Preface

or dismissive about the potential hardships and hazards of being dependent on having good survival seeds on hand when they themselves are lacking in the actual knowledge or experience to actually grow a survival garden from scratch on unamended soil. False and fatal hopes easily get reminded by nature who is not all that forgiving and luck can only go so far

This book was written in order to have an open optimistic discussion on the concept of "bug out" gardening. Building a garden in an area that is outside ones comfort zone and most likely has never been planted before.

I have noted as a longtime gardener, prepper, apocalyptic survival fiction and non fiction author etc. that we are seeing a proliferation of so called "Survival Seeds" being offered for sale by various vendors that seem to have inundated the survivalist and prepper community market. The majority of these offerings run the gamut of quality and selection but I would dare to say that the buyer and the seller mutually really don't know anything more about the seeds or specific varieties attributes other than that they are labeled "heirloom" "Non GMO" and maybe come in some nifty storage container that supposedly enhances long term storage.

There are many, many types and varieties encompassing a vast array of heirloom vegetable seeds that are available for sale. Each variety often times has pronounced differences in pest resistance, yields, and water requirements etc. in order to thrive that many buyers and sellers are fairly ignorant of, let alone informed and experienced enough or researched well enough to plausibly choose the best variety for the anticipated bleak bug out gardening environments we might visualize. They

Preface

tend to generalize the situation and forcibly apply a one size fits all selection.

I tend to call these overly hyped types of highly advertised survivalist romance lunacy oriented seed offerings "Seeds of Chance." You may as well say game of chance and I don't gamble on another mans game. I would rather stack the odds in my favor. Yes, there is a chance they might save you and then again there is a very good chance they won't. Whose deck of seed cards would you rather play with? Something you are holding in your hand that you created yourself that you recognize and are comfortable with, or a fresh pack of unknown casino seed seller house varieties sold to you for profit?

Yes, you might just find yourself lucky enough to raise a small, albeit, the vegetables produced will be a most likely stunted crop grown from you're over priced emergency survival seeds.

A chance as it were for you to feel lucky, maybe even blessed that you prepared by investing your hard earned money into a purchase to grow something for yourself and loved ones to eat in these hard times., That is, if you think you can manage to save yourself and your health long enough from societal collapse and everything else going on to hopefully see that the weather and bugs have cooperated with you to raise them to harvest. That would only occur in an already properly prepared garden soil most likely and of course that's sort of what goes on in everyone's gardens every year regardless of the state of affairs in the world.

Growing a garden is luck, hope and knowledge built upon access to resources and wisdom. I am not trying to scare you or belabor a point, I am just being realistic.

Preface

If you are already a dyed in the wool practicing gardener, then you have a feel for and a decided advantage about what it takes to nurture plants, if you are newbie or neophyte to the task thinking that you will just dig up your backyard and plant your survival seeds and be rewarded with a bounty, then you needs to think again because it just ain`t happening.

If you depend on the dig up the lawn and just haphazardly plant some vegetable seeds on your corner lot, then you will most likely be already dead long before even that enchanted and miraculous harvest time comes around that you have been expecting and dreaming about since you first bought that magical can of heirloom Non GMO survival seeds.

That is of course the key here, unless you have the luck of the cosmos on your side and have had the foresight and money to have purchased lots of food storage and had no dependence on growing anything what so ever, then maybe you might get yourself a shot at it again next year but then what?

You say that those magic beans are also for you try to bug out garden with no experience and a higher power will provide for you? Forget it, save the calories, the sweat, the tears and the misery; forget all about the chances of you running up on natural fertile soil in your bug out location or divine providence because that fanciful notion is probably not going to happen.

First off let me advise you that in the bigger scheme of trying to survive things natural and manmade, you shouldn't really need to be considering or buying any kind of special survival seeds at all and have sufficient

Preface

enough seed you have harvested personally with care and put back from trying to be more self reliant and raising a garden every year but that's not for everybody. But please, please start now and try to grow something, anything edible so you can get the practice and feel for growing plants.

If you have decided in your prepping or homesteading planning that you want to start or add on to an existing gardening plot of yours a more pest or disease resistant garden or maybe it could be that you want survival seeds for a last ditch recovery method or barter item later then by all means buy only the varieties that will work best in your area and do your own research both in the field and in the books.

Talk to other growers in your area to find out what varieties they like to grow and why, talk to the folks at the local seed and feed stores but be careful of the advice you get at the big box stores that offer mostly hybrids chosen by the nursery that sells them. Try to include in your preparations some of the seed variety selections that I will advise you to pick up or put aside as backups because of their special resilience to pests or diseases or that they possess a natural storage or nutritional specific attribute.

Bug out gardening or simply planting seeds in any barren patch of fresh untilled and un-amended soil is a fool's game at best but it can be done with some knowledge and a bit of foresight on your part. Remember that in a bug out situation your resources will be very scant and heavy or lightweight supply space for goods to be transported will be very limited.

For most of my demo or fictional scenarios I present I will have you relying on pretty much your wits

Preface

and an entrenching tool and a bucket to accomplish a task. I would like to go on record saying that this form of gardening no matter how many resources you have managed to accumulate on site or transport is a bad idea and unreliable in so many ways but in a survival environment you had best know and know well several ways to get it done.

That being said I will attempt to try to teach you a few of the simpler ways I have had success with growing on some of the worst soils I have ever seen in order to try to find a 'dry land" growing method or solution that will be simple and not labor intensive. Stress, reduced food intake, increased physical labor, responding to threats etc. will take enough toll on your body and mind and time spent doing anything other than surviving it all needs to be conserved.

I like to follow the lazy but wise mans gardening methodology under normal conditions and there are lots of reasons for you to let some weeds grow and not try to make your raised bed gardens look like they sit on a putting green. We aren't competing for no blue ribbons or doing things for appearance's sake anymore.

Dry land farming is an agricultural technique for non-irrigated cultivation of dry lands. I only use the term loosely here because I also plan on not having extra water resources available that I can rely on other than seasonal rain. Yes, quit objecting that you can hand water if you get close enough to a water source to haul buckets of the precious liquid from but we will get into that later. Water conservation still remains a primary important consideration even under these more ideal conditions and I am attempting to just spend my time growing and not hauling water to plants.

Preface

I can not stress enough to my readers that thinking you can create a garden big enough for yourself let alone others your first year on just any ground you grab to sustain yourself solely is a fantasy unless you are blessed with perfect conditions but I do have a formula that will get you by and minimally fed for quite sometime if you heed my advice.

I leave you with this quote from the Roman Era of great gardens and civilization and let us share its profoundness and meanings together as we shall examine this simple quote over and over again for new meanings as age, experience and life's strife encourages or reminds us that seeds and the nurture of them is life as we know it.

If you have a garden and a library, you have everything you need.
Marcus Tullius Cicero

Acknowledgements

http://www.gardentowerproject.com/

http://keyholefarm.com/

http://www.tomatocage.com/

1

THE CONCEPT OF A BUG OUT GARDEN

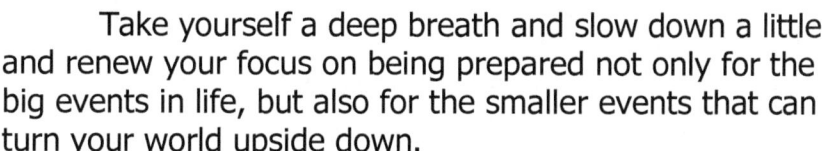

Take yourself a deep breath and slow down a little and renew your focus on being prepared not only for the big events in life, but also for the smaller events that can turn your world upside down.

Visualizing the need for something one might call a bug out garden is not as farfetched as one might think. Far from it, it is a survival skill set many of us wish to attain or sharpen. There are many foreseen and unforeseen RISK circumstances that might force you to leave your home and have to go start anew elsewhere, but preparing to garden immediately once you arrive at your destination seems to be a much overlooked or underserved topic in the preparedness community and this writer believes that preppers need to rethink and

THE CONCEPT OF A BUG OUT GARDEN

reevaluate their expectations and plans for coping with a long term disaster.

To survive life in general I say you need a garden, grid down we are all going to be farmers. Lose the focus on gun prepping and start prepping your soil and try to do some permaculture.

For that matter a lengthy list of Emergency management, homesteaders, farmsteaders and your average citizen will be well advised to heed my words in this opening statement because true basic preparedness lessons do not address this important subject and they pretty much leave you on your own after 72 hours except to repeat the same directions of store more for longer term survival if you expect a longer disaster.

Back in the civil defense era FEMA used to think about how to restart civilization and provided plans for things like converting a tractor over to a wood gasifier but they have abandoned planning in that direction just like they abandoned the fallout shelters that used to be available for every neighborhood.

There used to be in this country enough food stored in the form of grains etc in the National stockpile for every man woman and child to eat for 3 years. Now there is barely enough for a quarter of the population to survive a month. Are you getting the picture here? Does it strike home to you that while other countries are still building massive, sometimes small city sized underground bunkers for its populace we in somebody's great wisdom said that our shelters were a waste of money because everybody would been dead anyway in a nuclear exchange. Well even if they were correct in their assumptions what about natural disasters? I remember back in the 70`s the sirens

THE CONCEPT OF A BUG OUT GARDEN

went off indicating we had a tornado approaching. A bunch of folks in the neighborhood went to what was remembered to be the neighborhood shelter in the basement of a shopping center and milled around for a bit wondering who had the key to the thing and where were they at? Thankfully the tornado didn't touch down in that part of the city and inquiries and letters to the editor of the newspaper voicing concern that somebody had dropped the ball and not opened the shelter, soon revealed that all the shelters in the city had been closed for years and that was that.

No brilliant bureaucrats joining in the fray said let us in government start issuing keys, if we can find them, to the neighborhood watch or the fire department etc. Nope they were closed and you were on your own to shelter in place in your own residence or maybe your church's basement if it had one and you could rally everyone to come up with an emergency plan. We get the tail end of hurricanes blowing through my area every few years as close as we are to the Gulf that also spawn tornados in their wake but outside of go hide in the bathroom under a mattress and buy a weather radio we remain as unprepared as ever.

When so many good hardworking people today who are just one paycheck away from their own economic collapse the need to address personal preparedness becomes a subject not only for manmade and natural disasters but for everyday living. Many of us economically challenged, but aware individuals have enough anxieties about tomorrow and do what we can to prepare for basic needs like food and water for natural disasters but that is merely a very thin safety net that hopefully will last us until assistance arrives.

THE CONCEPT OF A BUG OUT GARDEN

The apprehensions of job loss, lack of retirement for a large majority of baby boomers, sickness, disability etc. makes all people at some time or another frustrated they can't save any money to offset those looming and very real risks but the money is just not there even after scrimping and saving and cutting back. What is wrong with everyone starting a victory garden like after WWII to get the country back on track and build a little food security?

One way to save is to grow a home garden and throw a buck or two into a mason jar every time you pick a few tomatoes or other vegetables you would have had to normally purchase at a premium from the grocery store. Most people might say they lack the land or resources for even this old standby of daily survival. Did you know you can buy seeds and plants on food stamps but you can't buy any kind of dirt, fertilizer or pesticides to grow them?

Sounds like quite a conundrum don't it and that other stuff gets expensive quickly, however, thankfully the community garden movement has in many places fixed that problem for you and offers you a plot of fertile dirt and the means to grow some of your own groceries if you are willing to take advantage of these private or public initiatives.

You would think that every community garden plot would be filled to capacity and every government housing project patio and back porch should be sporting pots of tomatoes or a potato barrel or something but they don't. Oh inside those tenement houses you will have lots of live non edible plants cheering up the atmosphere in many houses but somehow folks don't grasp that the means given to them to produce their own food should be their

THE CONCEPT OF A BUG OUT GARDEN

first priority in life and self-respectful survival attempts to better their station in life.

Growing an edible plant isn't really that difficult, we all got to probably experience the wonder of it all in grade school or something but as adults this idea of nurturing a seed and ourselves has somehow been forgotten.

People are living in a hand to mouth existence everyday and it took a bit of doing for the government to acquiesce and allow the purchase of vegetable seeds with food stamps while they distributed the government cheese but it's there now if some man or woman wishes to take a stand and be more self determinant and help provide for themselves.

Oh you might say having a tomato plant on your porch doesn't do much to help you save money and you surely can't live off of it as primary supplemental food prep or can you? How about a scenario where I have a fresh home grown tomato and you don't in one of those housing projects which during the growing season is most of the time I have one producing in several containers or in the dirt somewhere.

You buy tomatoes occasionally with your food stamps at the grocery store and I say "hey! I tell you what, next time you are going to the store to buy tomatoes get me some okra or flour or something in exchange and I will trade you for some maters?" Or maybe I am working in some menial paying office job and my coworkers say they would buy my surplus here and there so I can put a buck or two away in that mason jar? Could be all of us could get together at the community garden and start us a little vegetable and seed swapping

THE CONCEPT OF A BUG OUT GARDEN

biz. People do this type of business all the time overseas as a daily means of living but not so much here in the good old U.S.A. for a variety of reasons but lets look at what happens after a disaster.

The good hearted farmers and Grocery store chains donate surplus vegetables to feed those impacted by a hurricane or something and if they don't rot on the loading docks sitting around waiting to be distributed you might get some. In all my years responding to hurricanes I never heard of anyone saving some of those seeds or adding the rotten fruits and vegetables to the compost at the community gardens. That in my opinion is pretty screwed up but that is because we in the U.S. live in an affluent society that doesn't know how to encourage its citizens to assist in their own recovery or supplement government assistance. It wasn't always like this, we can point to victory gardens in WW II and can see the success of providing agricultural assistance in war torn or impoverished countries but we are very slow to recognize this type of self help disaster assistance needed here.

If you're on food stamps you're already in a personal disaster of magnitude and since you are in a financial disaster that means you can't get fertilizer and pesticides but if you can find transportation maybe then you can go get seeds. It is hard enough overcoming those last two items in the best of times but how about if you and your overpriced bug out bag is stuck out in the middle of nowhere and maybe even if say... you were lucky enough to pack the car with all the available food you had setting up house? Do you feel confident and ready? How long do you plan on lasting? What is your recovery plan?

THE CONCEPT OF A BUG OUT GARDEN

No nurseries or garden supplies for you, what are you going to do now? Most say they are not going to worry about it, the pioneers and wagon trains did the same thing. They loaded up and headed out to unplowed wild land and survived and you expect to do the same someway or perhaps something more modern but similar with that can of nitrogen packed survival seeds.

I think you kind of forgot that the early settlers had the gardening tools and seeds with them as well as the traditional and generational knowledge of growing stuff in a kitchen garden as part of the way of life back then to assist them that has mostly been forgotten by most today.

They also had draft animals to assist in the task of plowing and clearing land. Those same animals insured that fertilizer was available, they had hunting, and fishing and trapping skills that we can scarcely duplicate today but you got that survive-all modern bug out bag they didn't have so your chances for success are even better than theirs right? I guess you can already answer that question because you wouldn't be reading this book if you didn't and like many who have not progressed to your own preparedness and survival awareness level they will be seeking answers without resources or knowledge.

Society thrived in the 1800s for four very simple reasons: 1) a non-electric infrastructure already existed; 2) people had the skills, knowledge and tools to make do; 3) our population levels were far lower, and most people lived rural and raised a significant portion of their own food; and 4) there were relatively few people who didn't earn their way. To be blunt, if you didn't work, you seldom ate. Those who couldn't work (the disabled, the elderly,

THE CONCEPT OF A BUG OUT GARDEN

etc.) were cared for by family members or charitable institutions. There were no other options

Let us not go into extreme desolate grid down apocalyptic environments with preppers and their bug out bags heading for the woods for a moment, let us instead say you're an average family like those that evacuated from New Orleans from Hurricane Katrina and eventually ended up in a FEMA trailer park. Your house is gone, your job is gone, and you got 6 months to get your ducks in a row and get back on track before your case goes up for review before you get kicked out or they decide you can stay a bit longer.

They usually put these types of centers up on the outskirts of town so running to the store for every need becomes a gas as well as a financial ordeal in your circumstances. It sure would be nice if you had your old garden back that you been working on for years to help out but its underwater somewhere back where you used to call home after the levy broke and the chances of you ever moving back might not be an option. Well hey, I am a prepper and I brought with me my handy dandy survival seed pack so I will just scratch up some dirt outside my trailer and show everyone how a good prepper boy or girl can get by right? Wrong! Camp rules say you can't.

Ah hell, well let's go ask the officials if we can get assistance to dig up part of this cow pasture they got all these trailers parked on to make us one big humdinger of a community Victory garden!

That's the Ticket! We will show everybody by example how we are all going to pitch in together and overcome these hard times. Boy I bet the papers will love

THE CONCEPT OF A BUG OUT GARDEN

this and the farmers around here will pitch in and I can write about it in my survival preppers blog about how this is America facing a disaster at its best right?

Nope, wrong answer! The camp rules say you can't and that weird character of a security guard that you don't like added your name to his list of possible dissenters after you tried to make the media aware of this stupidity of letting land lay fallow when you and your neighbors just wanted to raise a community garden.

Crap! Ok, so that didn't work. Well I am going to take my FEMA visa card I finally got down to the local plant nursery and get me some potting soil, planter buckets and whatever else I need and line up pots on the side of my trailer full of tomatoes and edible flowers and such and show them folks. Ding! Ding! The doorbell announces a FEMA official who came to the door today and waved a contract at me I signed earlier when I moved in here. She gleefully tells me with a wry smile at my ignorance that absolutely no outside adornment of my trailer is allowed. She states most clearly that this rule applies in anyway including decorations for children's birthdays and Halloween. This fact of FEMA Camp living applies in any and everyway from Auburn And Alabama stickers or flags, to wind chimes and pink flamingo statues for the yard, so as far as she and the government is concerned that includes plants in pots or even adding my family name to the door or on a stake in front of my trailer.

That weird contracted security guard came with them and he is grinning over their shoulder that his advisement to me to put all that stuff I had just bought back in my car because it wasn't allowed is having a field

THE CONCEPT OF A BUG OUT GARDEN

day now cause after ignoring his ass I managed to get a few friends and neighbors to go on the same idiotic mission he was prepared to now make an example out of me on.

Foul I cry! Unfair, stupid and ignorant government red tape crap! Black demerit mark on my official "guest History" for me I guess, I get corrected for cussing in front of the FEMA official and the security guard smirks. I will protest I exclaim, I shall call an emergency meeting of the residents and get Washington on the phone I splutter as the weird guard starts fumbling for his chance to use his pepper spray on poor miscreant me.

He is not allowed to carry a gun on premises and I am not allowed to possess one either but thankfully no one has looked in my car trunk yet, but all persons and possessions on this place are subject to search so says the giant sign in front of this government facility and the contract I signed when moving in.

Take it up with the social workers the nice housing unit manger suggests while the FEMA official scowls. I will I claim, but I hope to be out of here long before they finally get around to scheduling a meeting.

Having no other resources or means to complain I start to say I will get this outrage put in the papers but then I remember that no outside charities or reporters are allowed on premises for any reason and shrug my shoulders at being screwed over once again.

Damn! Here comes the FEMA social worker telling me to calm down once again because I can be evicted for not following the rules or creating discord while the

THE CONCEPT OF A BUG OUT GARDEN

politically correct crowd is making sure they are not ignoring the jabbering easy street folks enjoying their own private classes on how not to be discriminated against and make the most of all the benefits big government has to offer.

Where is my special help or dedicated advisors and pencil pushers at for somebody that just wants to grow some food? When did just being a citizen become one thing while others became special in some way? I wondered out loud if the farmers' cooperative had any room on their back lot for me and the security guard suggested that I should try them and see if they also had trailer space I should be thinking about moving into, as a little crowd of officialdom and onlookers I attracted began to disperse.

This was a fictional account of a summary of several case studies I undertook for one of my master degrees in how to handle folks after a disaster, it was not adlibbed or expounded upon and such situations and regulations are trying to be addressed by academia and emergency management but that's been years ago and nothing has changed in any way to my knowledge.

Seeds and growing seeds to me as a means of sustenance and survival is a RIGHT and not a privilege but it says much for the state of affairs in this country.

The complaint my fictional FEMA park resident had has been voiced and documented many times but has not been brought to light or ever focused upon nearly as much as not allowing any outsiders at all be they charitable organizations, the church or even outside family members

THE CONCEPT OF A BUG OUT GARDEN

into these government controlled relocation and assistance housing centers.

They have their own law enforcement (contracted and federal) rules, regulations etc that stand apart from what is normally considered generally accepted constitutional rights.

Buy you a pack of heirloom seeds, hold on to them like its all you got in the world to assert your independence and freedoms with because that's what they are. Be aware that companies like Monsanto don't want you to have them and that government regulators side with the GMO lobbyists. And I tell you what, if you ever get stuck in a FEMA camp, start your one seed revolution and get out on the front porch and wave them at the security guards, it's not a gun it's an ideal. You are exhibiting your unalienable right to be able to find or grow food to feed yourself. Food is control; destiny is in your hands.

If you don't have the ability for yourself to attempt to grow a healthy nutritious vegetable now from the fruits of your own labors, question yourself and ask why? What is preventing me from doing this personally and legally?

No collecting rainwater in a few states anyone? Things are getting worse you just have to stop and notice. This is a freedom, just like your second amendment rights and ask yourself another question or questions, if I had nothing else but one pack of viable seeds and the knowledge to grow them to harvest, how far head and shoulders do I stand above the majority of my fellow survivors in a truly grid down survival situation,

THE CONCEPT OF A BUG OUT GARDEN

How would I fare if my house was burned down or I lost my job and I needed a bit of hope or a means to try to show I was improving myself or my circumstances without them?

Forget about romancing the pioneer days or living like in the late 1800`s,. Our Homes do not come equipped with outhouses, hand water pumps and a trained horse stabled in the back. Most people living today in this country don't have the faintest clue how to cook from scratch, much less grow or raise or harvest their own food.

Eighty percent of Americans live in cities and are fed by less than 2% which means farmers must mass-produce food for shipments to cities. And there are far too many people on multi-generational entitlement programs who literally know no other lifestyle except an endless cycle of EBT cards and welfare payments.

Having seeds for survival is a proactive positive measure, however incorporating them under less than ideal growing conditions takes a bit of thought and planning but we will review several methods that hopefully will increase your chances for success. Your best chance for success however is to gain experience by raising for yourself a small garden and see what works for your area. Gain real practical hands on experience before you need it.

There are a great many very good books on gardening or plant identification etc. available and I suggest you keep adding to your library because I am just giving you some basic gardening advice and this book is by no means meant to teach you more than a general understanding of planting methods.

THE CONCEPT OF A BUG OUT GARDEN

This author has been some kind of prepper/survivalist/homesteader or farmsteader for many years but he has yet to see anyone in these communities seriously address the subject of bug out gardening or address the need to be able to set up a quick emergency or kitchen garden on the fly as it might be referred to.

The reasoning for this he thinks is normally based on the flawed or ill-advised non gardener expectations held by many people that you can just put a vegetable seed in the ground, add water and it will somehow miraculously grow into something that can feed them one day.

The more experienced practicing gardeners who have had experience both nurturing the soil as well as various types of plants know different. They know it takes time, patience, physical energy and a bit of luck and wisdom to be able to successfully raise a successful crop every time.

We all know hopefully by now that if you are in a truly "Bug Out" scenario that you will have neither the time, energy, luck or patience needed most likely to expect any kind of productive results from the expenditure of precious calories creating a garden plot. Gardening is not likely to be very high on your list of tasks or worthy endeavors to undertake when faced with an immediate true survival situation goes without saying, yet most preppers get around to adding a selection of "survival seeds" to their bug out gear as an inevitable somehow necessary, smart or compelling thing to do.

THE CONCEPT OF A BUG OUT GARDEN

Well I can certainly understand this; to not eventually do this addition to your preparations is not being practical or to be acting decidedly foolish by not considering this measure. I myself have for many years had in someway or another dedicated reserved stash of seeds for emergencies that might occur from a manmade or natural disaster but overtime I lost any notion of "magical bean" dreams of a bountiful harvest from just their mere presence. My thoughtful and careful choosing of types and varieties won't help me if I am faced with poor growing conditions goes without saying.

No, the types of plants and vegetables I prepare to grow has changed many times over the years from various field trials as well as climatic and soil conditions changes and I have learned much from the experiences of what works and what doesn't.

When it comes to survival seed planning this author also has had the opportunity and chances to benefit from the barrage of newer or modified planting methods and containers that YouTube and various bloggers share to educate the public and expand the horizons of science and hobby farmers to try more productive or innovative methods. I learned what works and what doesn't through trial and error and will always consider myself still learning.

I have mentioned to you before that I considered myself a pretty astute survival seed planner, there are no formal degrees or courses for this but I am or was a formally educated and certified college grad of several university's in emergency management planning and administration although this has nothing to do with anything much about growing food. However, it does take

THE CONCEPT OF A BUG OUT GARDEN

into account the historical as well as the current demands of peoples' needs in a disaster.

A bad decision, a lack of awareness of culture or climate, a failure to account for special medical needs populations etc. can greatly affect how successful a food and water distribution to the affected populace is both planned and predicted.

Send the wrong food for humanitarian aid to the wrong foreign country or don't account for some people to have certain food allergies for example and you have not only compromised the people you are trying to save, but have compromised your mission and honor of the department and trust you serve.

That is what this book is about, making an informed decision about your own local or regional gardening preparedness strategies that are tailored to suit your own needs or family expectations. I am not a botanist, I am a southern prepper subsistence garden growing book author that has got his hands dirty most of his life come spring every year and knows a thing or two about survival in the woods and fields.

LESSON ONE TO TAKE AWAY

"SURVIVAL SEED" Packages and assortments all generally suck! There I said it, start throwing stones and fussing. If you want to die, disappointed, dejected and starving well then buy one of these so called professionally selected assortments for northern or southern climates and keep worshipping the gods of prepper survival media hype to feed you and your family.

THE CONCEPT OF A BUG OUT GARDEN

Have you ever tried to grow an ear of corn on even marginable soil? Most likely the majority of readers have not. Nor will they be ever forced to, hopefully. Most likely you don't even know how many ears of corn to expect per plant let alone how much area or support one space sucking water guzzling plant needs to produce anything approaching an edible effort.

Why in the hell all these so called survival seed bank B.S. offerings include various types of corn is beyond me other than it puffs up poundage for production and oh yea, acreage yield. They don't tell you how much wasted space you need to tend growing such a low yield per footage crop and they forget to tell you how to interplant other vegetables with it to increase yields.

Most of the so called expert growing instructions that come with those things will tell you nothing of a system of gardening used by Native American Indian Tribes for centuries utilized to create productive growing systems called "Three Sister Gardens" consisting of an inter-planting of corn, beans and squash. This was a symbiotic way of planting where by the beans produced or affixed nitrogen in the soil to grow the corn while the large leaves of the squash shaded out the weeds (reducing labor) and cooled the soil somewhat to help it retain water. The beans used the corn stalks as stakes to climb and support themselves as well as helped to keep the corn from being blown down in strong winds. No, this is not the direction or point of this book.

I will teach you that methodology as one of many survival planting methods for consideration later on in this book and you might be saying to yourself now, well if I just knew this bit of info those survival seed packs I got

THE CONCEPT OF A BUG OUT GARDEN

prepped are not such a bad value after all, nope you are wrong. That is unless you read one of my other books like the "Rural Ranger: A Suburban And Urban Trapping And Survival Guide" about using that corn seed as bait for a trap to catch squirrels or birds.

That would be a far better use for it in my opinion than trying to dig up by hand a huge section of ground to plant this way, how many squirrels or quail per acre do you think it's going to take for you to replace the calories you are going to expend clearing land and tending that stuff for 3 months until it might be ready to eat if you didn't have a drought or a plague of locusts come to visit?

You got to follow me here, I know it's tough, your heart, your soul and your prepper mind went into choosing just the right 'survival seed' garden package you decided to purchase and me putting it down is making you lose focus. It does have its uses and several of the selections in it might be fine as some temporary insurance or assurance.

It is your HOPE, the great mythical dream, your mainstay, your its all I have outlook that things might get better one day and even if you admit you're a bit disillusioned or optimistic about that survival seed pack saving your butt, it still makes you feel good that at least you got some seeds when others won't even have access to such a treasure in the hard times to come will give the advantage you seek.

Man, you got to get over that idea and quickly, those seeds might well get you killed for believing in them too much and for what? So you could be seen doing something, well just about anything, to have a positive

THE CONCEPT OF A BUG OUT GARDEN

outcome for you and your family that somewhere deep down in your heart of hearts most likely you realize will be a failure without some divine intervention?

It is better than nothing you might be heard saying and that is truer than you know at this point, but you must understand you and your preparedness or survival gears' limitations just like you do with all the rest of that crap you have researched and fretted over and eventually bought to put into your bug out bag and you also probably broke the bank doing so. Say it with me now, knowledge weighs nothing, costs little, it's hard to lose and is the basis of all survival regardless of expenditures.

"Oh no, many might say, it is just way too much more work to have to think about studying and understanding every variety of seed and growing condition. This whole prepping acquisition of knowledge thing is wearing on my mind already and I continue to study some about the difference of the varieties of vegetables contained in that survival seed purchase I made. I bought your book didn't I?"

Look for example you might say these Great Lake Beans produce well under my conditions the package and internet says and I would respond with my agreement that under ideal conditions they were a very worthy and tasty variety for consideration to plant if you understood their growth requirements.

Those types of beans need strong staking or a trellis, which means you need string, poles etc., why don't you consider a bush type bean that doesn't require that resource and physical labor like the bush variety of bean called Contender.

THE CONCEPT OF A BUG OUT GARDEN

Well, you might say I never heard of that one but I will give it a try one day, but around here we always have grown that type and it gives us loads of beans to which I would reply, sure they produce well but I get almost double the amount of beans with Contender and with no staking or maintenance. They produce a drought and bug resistant truck garden crop that is more dependable doing it my way and with less work.

A 10x4 raised bed of Contender beans that you buy seeds from your local seed and feed store will start producing in 40 days and keep you and your family in beans all season. Succession crops can also be planted. These are as close to magic beans as you can get and will out produce everything else in the garden. The price continues to go up on these but at $6 a pound in my area they are a bargain and I always keep a couple pounds on hand. It takes about a ¼ pound or more to plant a 10x4 area. Get you some!

COMPANION PLANTING THE OLD FASHIONED WAY WITH A 3 SISTERS GARDEN
corn, pole beans & squash

THE CORN SUPPORTS THE BEANS, THE BEANS ADD NITROGEN AND THE SQUASH SHADES OUT THE WEEDS

1) Plant the corn after danger of frost has passed.
2) Plant the pole beans when the corn is 5 inches high.
3) Plant squash seeds one week later.

IMAGE CREDIT: MOTHER EARTH NEWS

Well you might say, I needed me a climbing and vining variety so my wife can try out that three sister gardening thing you were speaking about, I wanted a pretty much strngless bean that was a bit cold hardy for my area. My response would be have you ever tried it? I did the Great Lakes Bean thing, wrong variety for a Three Sisters Garden, they are prolific viners that will close the leaves of the biggest corn plant and mat up and form a

THE CONCEPT OF A BUG OUT GARDEN

sail for the wind to hit and drag down all that shallow rooted corn and create one hell of a mess to try to rescue and deal with. I also thought it was cool that down here in the Deep South the grasshoppers liked to hang out on them and only eat the beans and leave the rest of my garden alone! I know what to plant for the locusts coming my way now!

I thought about using them as sort of a throwaway companion plant to attract the destructive bug once they were drawn away from the rest of my gardens. Seems they are some sort of gourmet weed hopper.

If you have the time, inclination and knowledge to shop around for another company's survival seed packet offering other than mine from someone other than mine then by all means do so, if you want my one stop, and highly considered offerings as an economically priced convenience then buy from me after researching this books contents and knowing what you're doing, enough said.

KingsMountainSeeds.webs.com

STEP TWO TAKE AWAY

THE CONCEPT OF A BUG OUT GARDEN

Get the concept of bugging out and/or creating the ultimate bug out bag out of your head, I and many other writers like me have told you for years that this is a bad almost suicidal decision to leave your home and go to the great unknown that gets way too much focus in the prepper community at large. You are simply not going to make it, you don't even have the skills to go from point A to point B yet and instantaneously provide, sustain and begin growing yourself a food crop whenever you get there regardless of what ever self-assured level of prepperdom knowledge you might have already achieved at this point unless you have somehow become a student of history or pioneer perseverance to know what everyone knew back then to forage or bring crops with them to sustain a new life. You need to be able to create a new sustainable existence in this world and gardening is where you start.

The generations before us and the great explorers and forefathers of agriculture and civilization in the world were not bereft of what it took to sustain an expedition and planned accordingly with much aforethought. They provisioned great tall sailing ships for long journeys, the go west young man settlers did the same with their Conestoga wagons of the plains to grow something food wise to sustain them.

Were they visionaries? One might say so, because they somehow knew that the seed and plants of known varieties they were used to and brought with them might not be available for their planting once they arrived at their destination.

Others who have gone before me knew that supply lines were short or non-existent and thought to provide a

THE CONCEPT OF A BUG OUT GARDEN

resource, a locally produced product and a means of business to sustain themselves and others in their new environment. While still most others knew spring was for planting and the only thing they could depend on was planting in these new worlds.

That is another thing my prepper friends, it takes agricultural grains like wheat and barley to sustain a civilization but this book will not address that fact or aspect. The Bible please note says that "wheat is the staff of life" if that is true then why is it no other prepper to my knowledge addresses this basis of true historic civilization fact besides me?

I already know it takes a community and a lot of cleared land to raise such a crop so therefore it is inherently flawed to even suggest or attempt to reason it out or explain its growing nature as a solution of sustenance in a bug out situation unless I point out reserving a can of it for planting versus eating it someday far from the original day you arrive at a mythical bug out location. Don't be expending time and energy adding ammo to your stores to protect a can of food but instead think about how to get the community to plant and defend it.

No, my friend, what you need to do for yourself is what is called nowadays consume one of the newly rediscovered super foods. Plants that have attributes and medicinal qualities far exceeding traditional diets Americans have become accustomed to are called super foods because they are the most nutritionally dense plants known to man. As a kid raised in the 60's and 70`s with various back to the earth hippie and commune movements going on I got to see a lot of agricultural efforts and

THE CONCEPT OF A BUG OUT GARDEN

changes as well as dream of personally achieving some unattainable peace and love utopia I planned on creating for myself someday.

I had very little illusions regarding that traditional deep south "Truck Farming" was a risky and laborious undertaking subject to the fickle fates of weather, droughts, insects, disease and economics but like everyone else engaged in the whole back to the earth movements back then in its infancy and glory days to gladly be swallowed up with the hype and visions of being self reliant whole heartedly envisioning hopes and dreams of success of doing it all on my own or finding others to share my visions with to seek support and labor from.

There is a big difference and hard lessons to be learned when someone "follows their dreams" to be self-sustainable in a modern world with or without working faucets, electricity and a corner seed and feed store in a crap has hit the fan situation.

Poor will make you a farmer, a skinny and tired one, food is a necessity you that do for yourself because no one else will; poor will make you a smart farmer that knows about subsistence living at its worst.

You find yourself able to eat edible weeds instead of spending money to eradicate them because you need to sell the tomatoes you have grown to pay the water bill and calculate what they cost to grow and make a few cents to do this task with trepidation and more sweat with fewer results. You learn the land, what grows better in one place or can be found thriving elsewhere for no other reason than it seems it wanted to grow there that way and duplicate it.

THE CONCEPT OF A BUG OUT GARDEN

You can sort of begin to recognize the soil problems in other peoples garden plots having less success by the weeds it grows or the diseases plants get like blossom end rot in tomatoes and squash for lack of calcium and amend it cheaply with something natural like saving egg shells instead of buying an overpriced soil amendment from a garden center you don't have the money to consider to spend anyway and the bastards decided to write it in Latin so you couldn't figure it out when you read the listed ingredients on the label of anyway of what it was made with they are trying to bilk you into thinking it was some kind of miraculous cure only their trademark name possessed.

You want to know how to get by in hard times?

Study if you will an example of finding the poorest old person you know that is getting by in the country on a tiny piece of land and seems to be as healthy as they can be without any medical care or state assistance and you will be amazed at the humbleness and resourcefulness you lack; I still do this. Once these people and this knowledge is past, it is gone. Learn now from your grandparents and old folks in your community before their wisdom and wit is gone.

Folks don't have to be poor to be resourceful; they can just be transplants or following dreams of adventure or self reliance. Talk to a variety of people that have moved from different parts of the country and compare notes on how they find gardening different in your locale and how things were historically done back in their state. Lots of times they have brought seed or plants with them

THE CONCEPT OF A BUG OUT GARDEN

you're unfamiliar with. Maybe they have some new gardening tips and tricks for you.

This is me visiting my 92 year old neighbor buddy Frank who moved from the backwoods of Maine to the sticks of Alabama a little over 15 years ago to bless our little community. He parked a travel trailer and built a porch on it to get away from the snow and taxes and enjoy some southern small home living before anybody else even thought of it. Frank grows amazing white and yellow roses and gives me and my girlfriend very wise and insightful history lessons when I sneak by to share an adult beverage and watch the sun go down occasionally. Yes "Snowbirds "will always be welcome in Dixie even if they are jokingly considered damn Yankees! He always though reminds me "As Maine goes so goes the Nation!"

THE CONCEPT OF A BUG OUT GARDEN

Many times whatever variety of plants they are growing is gone from the seed catalogues, lost to history or no longer offered by corporate seed sellers because these folks don't frequent the garden clubs and spring and summer hybrid plant stores that spring up at the big box store world we have become entirely too dependent upon to engage in our favorite hobbies of gardening. No our choices of what to grow especially for those that haven't been a part of summer, spring and winter gardening as a lifestyle become narrower and narrower as plant patents and trends over take our available seed selections. Talk to your neighbors that grow or join a seed sharing club on the internet and be amazed at being able to preserve or grow something that used to be always available but for some reason (Think Corporate Money) is no longer available to be the already discovered cure all to your gardening ills. What was good enough for Grand dad and Grand Ma is often times even better and good enough for me than a hybrid that just came out to mimic an old strain proven to produce without the killer gene of a GMO to not to be able save seeds from because they become sterile after one season or the non dependable to reproduce true hybrid.

It is a sink or swim world of failure and fertilizer dependant food for us with this odd array of unrecognizable offerings and I bet most people that are reading this book for the first time can't pick one main crop to sustain themselves with over another.

The old time subsistence gardeners are neither to be elevated upon the chair of survival nor be diminished by their lack of wits, ingenuity or economics to elevate

THE CONCEPT OF A BUG OUT GARDEN

their lot when considering these so called antiquated wisdoms most people in their day possessed.

It's all they know, it is what has always been there for generations to survive on and sustain them reliably and that is what you look at with a jaded eye and acceptance that Lord knows for whatever reason, it works, and study that segment judiciously.

Broad leaf leafy greens at all seasons plays a part, perennials sometimes depending on climate or seasons, ask them old folks what is a cash crop, that's something you can grow easily and have a bit left over and be prepared for that nice conversation that you were having with them up to this point to be all the sudden reduced to suspicion and lack of tangible information.

This knowledge is what sets them apart from others suffering their strife and economic imbalance and it can be jealously guarded and protected as the only hope they have and means to hold their head up with some bit of pride.

The hope is they can support and sustain themselves better than you, to feel like they are some how better than you if you're an outsider, to be more successful and better their lot through sales or knowledge in the community that they know a bit more, it is their prestige or whatever, thing is, given a plot of land and their resourcefulness most anywhere they survive and continue to survive in many cases with nothing more than a general store that the proprietor somehow gives them credit for purchases of what they can't produce that they exist naturally as a part of this great nation like generations before them doing the same things. True

THE CONCEPT OF A BUG OUT GARDEN

survivors for generations to come and true knowledge their heirs used to possess to carry on and enjoy this subsistence way of living.

Can you honestly say that you can do that? I didn't say be happy doing it, I said live this way and produce by any means and by hook or crook enough extra goods, be it from growing something or working odd jobs to pay your bills at the local store and hold your head high, that you are not owing anything to anybody, well not much anyways and saving a mite for a rainy day or when you get hurt?

Of course you can't, I can't either because this world and technology is changing at such a rate no one can keep up so I kind of personally decided I would revert to the old style living on a scorched earth with woes, myself dependent only on what I could put into it and not expect much out of it until this hard living and land was mastered.

What a man needs in gardening is a cast-iron back, with a hinge in it. ~Charles Dudley Warner, My Summer in a Garden, 1871

STEP 3

Look at your hopes and dreams like a survival packet of seeds. That is by far the hardest conceptual statement I have been forced to describe as a writer but the most important and profound realization I have come to as a prepper. It requires knowledge to raise a seed or attain a goal. Somewhere since this is my intro to my book and my ramblings I will teach you why you would trade that whole big expensive bug out bag of yours for 12

THE CONCEPT OF A BUG OUT GARDEN

bucks worth of Sun choke tubers that would sustain you the rest of your life and quit trying to buy bug out bag giz whizzes that are already giving you a sense of personal economic collapse.

Hey, just for fun go read or listen to on Audible.com my Possum Prepping book or Rural Ranger to learn that you already have all the tools you need to survive in your kitchen drawer if you just knew how to use them.

"Don't judge each day by the harvest you reap but by the seeds that you plant."
Robert Louis Stevenson

THE CONCEPT OF A BUG OUT GARDEN

I don't expect you to get the full meaning of that last statement yet in order to put on you on the road to prepperdom or farmsteading through real life acquisition of individual survival knowledge but we are getting there.

I wrote a book awhile back in 2003 called the Rural

Ranger that taught some skills of hunting and trapping to live off the land, I wrote another one more recently called "Possum Prepping", so you could live in these economically challenging times and have hope for the future but no volume of my country boy lore could better prepare you for the abyss of societal breakdown and collapse as well as the uncertain future of old age and

THE CONCEPT OF A BUG OUT GARDEN

uncertain economics as what I foresee in my own backyard and this appeal for you to consider.

The soil is the great connector of lives, the source and destination of us all some day. It is the healer and restorer and resurrector, by which disease passes into health, age into youth, and death into life. Without proper care for it we can have no community, because without proper care for it we can have no life. ~Wendell Berry, The Unsettling of America: Culture and Agriculture

CAN YOU TAKE JUST YOUR SURVIVAL SEEDS AND START A NEW LIFE, NOT AS YOU KNOW IT NOW, BUT JUST DAILY CONTINUE TO SURVIVE WITH WHAT YOU CAN CARRY IN ONE HAND AND SEE IT THROUGH?

A bold and reckless statement to consider be assured, a philosophy, a statement of awareness of your environment and preparing for it as a prepper summarized. Great kings and governments way back in the past were forced to send out expeditions to find alternatives to failing crops, chronic starvation in their populace, new economic opportunities, new medicines etc. for centuries and this knowledge is the basis for all our history as well as mankind's attempt to change his environment.

THE CONCEPT OF A BUG OUT GARDEN

With all our great technological advances in communications, the knowledge bases of the internet to get instant info on anything at a press of a button and keyword there remains no better survival tool than a person that is adapted to the land and has the wisdom and seeds to be able someday to forgo hunting and gathering and become a model agriculturally based civilized society that doesn't war over land and petroleum based resources.

Think upon that statement "One looks back with appreciation to the brilliant teachers, but with gratitude to those who touched our human feelings. The curriculum is so much necessary raw material, but warmth is the vital element for the growing plant and for the soul of the child."
Carl Jung

You got anything in that bug out bag or consider the bag itself for that matter that wasn't produced by an oil based technology except those survival seeds you have that mostly takes animal crap to grow versus petrochemicals you don't have?

Can you identify any roots, nuts and berries to sustain yourself until you can grow a crop? Most likely no. don't forget the potato was unknown in Europe until stolen from the Incas, don't forget the Irish starved because of English politics and the stupidity of folks growing one crop and one variety when a natural blight hit.
What did the Irish people eat for thousands of years before the potato was introduced? Who is still around to remember? How about for hundreds of years the botanists of the day called the common garden tomato

THE CONCEPT OF A BUG OUT GARDEN

"Devils apple" and everyone living then knew not to eat it because it was considered poisonous?

Where did these people living in these times get their information from? The church, the government, the scientists, that said to remain healthy, listen to us? Reminds me of the current European Union not allowing curved or overly large cucumbers to be sold in Britain these days, but it is all right to sell a new blue strawberry GMO enhanced by fish genes to grace your dinner plate.

Hell, they ain`t got to deny you food to subjugate you, you will grow it yourself to kill yourself in hopes of becoming more healthy with eye appeal if you don't accept that this is a multicultural world that accepts new colors! Hell, I thought those blue strawberries were cool until my research said that the Chinese supposedly NON GMO seeds were GMO and wondered what eating fish and strawberries were all about! Supposedly it's more cold hardy because they used an arctic fish, then they tweaked it with whatever creature they could make or produce to give you the electric blue pleasing color of an acid trip but that don't harm you they say so folks buy some.

I pretty much thought it was just neat to have a high priced new colorful veggie to sell to the Hilton Hotel up the road but when I looked at the new offering of a BLACK strawberry I had to wonder at the sensibility of it all let alone that I think strawberries should be red if you are going to get me to eat one! I wonder if years from now we are going to end up with Smurf people that like those things and blame it on their consumption.

Plant rights, seed laboratory patent rights, bull shit I say, how about the basic human right to feed ones' self,

THE CONCEPT OF A BUG OUT GARDEN

I need a fishing permit to eat, sea oats are an endangered species illegal to pick so I don't eat them, mercury poisoning in wild caught fish is acceptable based on FDA studies but I got to pay taxes and subject my property to regulatory stateside commissions to inspection while millions of human waste produced farm raised shrimp from Asia are my only affordable grocery store option for seafood.

If you think in terms of a year, plant a seed; if in terms of ten years, plant trees; if in terms of 100 years, teach the people.
Confucius

THE CONCEPT OF A BUG OUT GARDEN

"The fact that we have to fight for something so essential to life as the integrity of seeds, speaks to the real drama of this present time: that we have to fight to preserve what is most fundamental and sacred to life."
—Llewellyn Vaughan-Lee
from "Seeds and the Story of the Soul"

    Anyone reading this old man's book of prepper planting tricks remember their elementary school history lessons of the infamous Captain Bligh of an English ship in Her Majestys Navy that was collecting breadfruit in the tropics to be possibly grown in Britain or the colonys and the mutiny that ensued by the vitamin C deficient crew

THE CONCEPT OF A BUG OUT GARDEN

eating salt pork to jettison the cargo in protest of lack of food, water and extra work taxing their strength?

Not a man on the ship and most folks then and now can tell you what the disease scurvy is or how to treat it except take a vitamin C capsule in these modern times or your teeth will fall out.

Hell, drink a few cups of pine tree tea needles for the natural Vitamin C and get over it a lot of us more back to the woods folks know but for some reason that is not in the common knowledge base most of us modern minds realize. To die for superstition or government policies is ridiculous and only occurs when religion or politics get organized to control the so called ignorant populace.

There used to be root beer stand franchises everywhere way back in the day but government says sassafras causes liver damage so they outlawed its cheap production and replaced it with whatever chemical most closely reproduced the flavor of the original or changed the label to gourmet, the same reason pink sludge can be sold as a chicken nugget I guess.

Whatever happened to its safe, it's natural and probably won't hurt you? Hell, peanut better which saved thousands and thousands of poor school children is getting banned in schools because the 1 in a million will get violently sick if they eat it.

I am going to tell you about many plants like this in my book and I assume no responsibility for this advice, it is yours to do the research and know if it is safe or not for your diet but please observe the warnings I do commit to you.

THE CONCEPT OF A BUG OUT GARDEN

For example, I know eating Poke (Latin) or as the old time poke salad (actually the word is Salat) as the song goes talking about somebody named Annie still graces the plates of many a southerner requires special cooking to remove its toxic properties but I eat it and depend on it as well as being vastly familiar with it.

How many times does someone have to tell you to change the water twice as you cook it because it could bother you or do you need to be reminded constantly in my directions before it reminds you of my warnings?

It is not difficult, neither is it for me to tell you to only gather new shoots because they taste better, not as bitter and contain less of the toxin you have been changing the water for, just like your mom taught you. Polk greens taste buttery without butter, there you have it. I like them and they are good for me, if I observe a little caution and avoid over indulgence. You never over indulge in anything or haven't we learned that yet? Especially if it comes with some kind of warnings?

The reason we are going down this rabbit hole of so called bug out gardening will be different for many people but the precept is the same, we want to know the hows and the whys of how to grow the most food possible in the smallest amount of space available as quick as we can.

Believe me, I understand taste matters and so did our ancestors that could look at a barren pasture and know there was a bounty to sustain them if they could just stomach it and had their favorite plants that they tamed and civilized to their use from wild grasses like corn and wheat or whatever. It dang sure beats eating bugs for

THE CONCEPT OF A BUG OUT GARDEN

protein or raising chickens to eat the bugs if eventually somebody figured it all out first and I can learn from them. I bet those folks had hot sauce and other flavorings stored like every soldier and otherwise has available to make a monotonous diet better. Grow you some herbs too if I haven't mentioned it yet, dandelion greens might be dandy and you might be crazy for kale but salt, pepper, vinegar, oregano anything beats thinking you can get goat like tendencies to eat whatever daily without new flavorings to break up that monotony. An old saying is a little bit of sugar makes the medicine go down. Enough of anything if it is a change and not over powering is a welcome addition to say a diet of beans and rice if you were lucky enough to have prepped those and when it comes to eating totally greens they seem to take on the flavor of grass. I will fight you over that one can of bacon I have left!

Hell, in Alabama they still have certain kinds of a variety of geese called Toulouse that won't eat vegetables and are also used for weeding cotton without the use of herbicides. I am also a student of history and modern advancements so take what I have to say and look for your own solutions found from personal research once you establish your own starting point.

At the moment, I am teaching you from the perspective that you already have way too many hopes and thoughts of that pack of survival seeds you bought and what to do with them before you are challenged to see the first sprout in a post-apocalyptic world. The times they are a changing; and me, I am going back in times and methodologies with an occasional modern twist or adaptation to insure a successful harvest.

THE CONCEPT OF A BUG OUT GARDEN

"Ordinary seeds need the right combination of soil, water, and climate to grow. Once those conditions are in alignment, the seed will naturally begin to develop. The seed of Buddha Nature is the same. It will lie dormant until the right conditions come together. But once we discover this potential within us, we can water our seed with loving kindness and prepare its bed with mindfulness. When we do so, the growth of the seed of awakening will be effortless and natural."
—Acharya Judy Lief
from "A Little Seed of Awakening"

2

DIG IN AND FERTILIZE!

DIG IN AND FERTILIZE!

Bill Gates: 'I'm Obsessed With Fertilizer'

From an op-ed written by Microsoft co-founder Bill Gates for Wired.com:

"I am a little obsessed with fertilizer. I mean I'm fascinated with its role, not with using it. I go to meetings where it's a serious topic of conversation. I read books about its benefits and the problems with overusing it. It's the kind of topic I have to remind myself not to talk about too much at cocktail parties, since most people don't find it as interesting as I do.

But like anyone with a mild obsession, I think mine is entirely justified. **Two out of every five people on Earth today owe their lives to the higher crop outputs that fertilizer has made possible.** It helped fuel the Green Revolution, an explosion of agricultural productivity that lifted hundreds of millions of people around the world out of poverty.

These days I get to spend a lot of time trying to advance innovation that improves people's lives in the same way that fertilizer did. Let me reiterate this: A full 40% of Earth's population is alive today because, in 1909, a German chemist named Fritz Haber figured out how to make synthetic ammonia."

Pretty profound words I would say. Mr. Gates has an understanding, he gets "IT", and he is a survivor.

First off we are going to assume you the reader has got some survival seeds on hand already or your research wouldn't have directed you into buying this particular book

DIG IN AND FERTILIZE!

of mine and approach to disaster gardening. Let's maximize this premise while we theorize that no matter how good the seeds you have on hand are that you will require soil nutrients to grow them so we will first focus on fertilizer.

There are a couple ways to approach this based on your ability to haul supplies and the funds you might have available. Most preppers would prefer we talk about lack of space and lack of funds first but either way you go, the expense is nominal and the space your supplies will take up is as minimal as you wish to make it with my methodology. It all depends on your goals and what you are preparing for.

Many commercial fertilizers are available in different nutrient grades and analysis. Unless you're fairly new to gardening, you've likely seen the three numbers listed on the label of the majority of premixed fertilizers. If you aren't familiar with what they mean, the numbers represent nitrogen, phosphorus, and potassium or N – P – K. These vital nutrients are needed for strong aerial growth, root development, and overall plant health, respectively.

A good way to remember N – P – K is by using the phrase "Up, down, and all around." Knowing these three main components is essential to creating the perfect food for your garden. State laws require that the label on all fertilizers sold show a guaranteed amount of nitrogen (N), phosphorus (P_2O_5), and potassium (K_2O). A nutrient analysis of 10-20-10 means it is guaranteed to contain 10 percent N, 20 percent P_2O_5, and 10 percent K_2O.

DIG IN AND FERTILIZE!

I can throw a 50 lb bag of a good complete fertilizer like 10-10-10 in my trunk for about 30 bucks and feel well prepared to start me a crisis garden most anywhere.

10-10-10 Granular All Purpose Fertilizer Application Rates:

10 lbs. per 1000 sq. ft. = 1 lb. of N per 1000 sq. ft. 500 lbs. per acre = 50 lbs. of N per acre.

So an area of a 10x100 ft would only need 10lbs if you're going by formula. Most likely you are not going to make a long narrow swath like this but it's easy to envision 10ft wide by 10 ft wide (100 sq ft) and you can get 10 plots this size out of 10lbs of fertilizer.

Seems crazy doesn't it to only have to put 1lb per 100 square feet but that's the formula. REPEAT AFTER ME: DO NOT APPLY TOO MUCH FERTILIZER!

You can cause yourself more harm than good and hey I and many others have done so thinking it didn't matter and maybe my excess would yield better results if it was only economy to be considered.

I get into different formulas and application rates later in the book as well as the why fors and why nots but for now lets say your just growing space conscious of packing your vehicle for a bug out.

A 50 lb bag doesn't take up that much space flattened out in the trunk. If you used that bag of fertilizer in your car's trunk judiciously and prudently you could get

DIG IN AND FERTILIZE!

5 crops out of a 1000 sq ft area. This is a large garden and will take some keeping up with.

Fertilizer labels are very misleading, implying that plants need high amounts of just NPK - plants need many more nutrients than NPK, and they need very small amounts of each. For example I don't just want N-P-K alone - I very much prefer to include some calcium in there so I save eggshells or I can buy bone meal, etc. to add to the mix.

The heart of the question is really when you look at fertilizers is, "how much of each nutrient does a plant need?" The answer is shockingly little. Only tiny amounts of each nutrient are actually removed from the soil when we harvest the vegetable garden. We're talking grams of each nutrient. If your soil is poor and losing nutrients through leaching and volatization, then we need to add us a little more than if we have a balanced, sustainable ecosystem, but not nearly as much as one might think.

In addition, the chance that your plants and soil will be happy with 10-10-10 fertilizer on its own is very low - plants prefer their nutrients in organic form, prepared by microbes.

A "complete fertilizer" only has to supply the three NPK nutrients. We know, of course, that plants need many dozens of nutrients (perhaps over 70), so it makes no sense to apply only three. In fact, applying too much of these three indiscriminately often causes more problems than benefits which we will discuss later. Also you do a side dress application after the first general soil amendment. This often works out to one tablespoon per square foot.

DIG IN AND FERTILIZE!

Total nitrogen (residual and fertilizer) needed by various vegetables and timings for side dress application.		
Vegetable	*Total nitrogen needed*	*Side dress application timing**
	Pounds nitrogen/ 1,000 sq ft*	
Asparagus***	1.7	
Beans (snap, bush)***	1.4	
Beans (pole)	2.3	2-3 weeks after emergence when leaves are expanding, prior to flowering
Broccoli and Cauliflower	4	4 weeks after transplantation and again when head development is initiated; if secondary shoots are desired, fertilize again after first head is harvested
Carrot	3	6-8 inches tall
Celery	4.1	Weekly
Cucumber	3.4	When vines start to run and after first harvest
Eggplant	4.6	First fruit 1 inch long
Lettuce	4.6	Weekly
Onion (bulb)	3	Weekly after plants are 1/4 inch in diameter; 8 weeks after emergence

DIG IN AND FERTILIZE!

Onion (bunching)	2.8	Same as bulb onions
Pepper	3.2	4 weeks after transplanting, prior to flowering; after first harvest
Potato	4.5	Beginning bloom
Pumpkin	3	Second true leaf; vines begin to run
Radish***	1	
Spinach	2.3	3 weeks after emergence
Squash (summer)	3.4	Second true leaf; first fruit and winter sets
Sweet Corn	3.6	12 inches tall
Tomato	4.6	12 inches tall; first fruits are 1 inch in diameter

*If there will be more than one side dress application, divide the remaining nitrogen evenly and apply accordingly.
**1,000 sq ft = an area 20 feet by 50 feet, 25 feet by 40 feet, or 30 feet by 33.3 feet.
***Nitrogen requirements will be satisfied after preplant applications.

You might be thinking to yourself somewhere at this point OH NO! I got to get more stuff and its going to take up more space and cost me more money!

No it's not, just settle in and listen a bit, it kind of goes with the flow of putting you in a bug out gardener

DIG IN AND FERTILIZE!

mindset. I just listed the aforementioned commercial stuff for convenience and academics.

You actually have all sorts of fertilizer waiting on you wherever your bug out location is at, but you do want to bring along some green thumb growing enhancers with you. Don't worry, they are cheap and compact and can be had for a reasonable price at any grocery store.

Matter of fact I will teach you how to make a bug out garden bucket (BGB) out of a normal sized galvanized one or you might want to try a bigger 5 gallon plastic one later on.

They both weigh the same, however, there are distinct advantages to using different containers, matter of fact I suggest putting a galvanized pail inside of your 5 gallon bucket for reasons that will become apparent later. The contents of this kit are basically the makings for homemade Miracle Grow and some bug sprays etc. to help insure your success.

The materials found on site to grow a garden are plentiful and one of the best fertilizers arrives the moment you do in the form of urine.

That's right good old human pee, sounds gross but it is not. Urine is an excellent homemade fertilizer for plants and soil. Urine is sterile. Use it neat (think the word means undiluted like a shot of whiskey) or diluted, as long as you are not sick or carrying a virus or some other communicable disease.

It is also a popular compost activator. Pour it on because it's loaded with nitrogen as well as potassium and

DIG IN AND FERTILIZE!

phosphorous. The nitrogen is in the form of urea which is the ideal form for soil uptake and fertilizing plants.

Urine

The average adult produces about 1 1/2 quarts of urine per day. Diluted 1:20 with water, this would make about 7 gallons of high-nitrogen liquid fertilizer, so a family of four could produce enough high-nitrogen fertilizer to produce an average garden and lawn.

As the scientist Brinton suggests, when we think of N-P-K, we should also think N-Pee-OK! You might keep a designated bale of hay out in the garden for urine deposits. If you do this you can use the urine-enriched hay from "pee bales" as nutrient-rich mulches in your garden.

You can pee in a bottle or bucket, dilute it 20:1 with water, and then feed the plants or your lawn directly.

Ways you can use urine in the garden:

You can pee directly in the garden, too, I have often. Just make sure you don't pee right on your plants – ever notice how certain shrubs or patches of grass in dog parks turn yellow and die? It's not a great homemade lawn fertilizer, that's for sure – that is unless you dilute it first so think clear is cool and any other color needs second thoughts if direct from the source.

Urine should be used as fresh as possible to fertilize your plants, but if that's not always possible, put a lid on the jar or container immediately. Urine that's been left in the air for a while will be busy converting itself from urea

DIG IN AND FERTILIZE!

into pure ammonia — your compost pile will still love it though.

For pouring around the roots of your vegetables and other plants, dilute 1 to 10 with water (**keep a handy watering can near the back door).** You should already be thinking about where you most often go at inopportune times, the call of nature will remind you that you don't like venturing far in early mornings and late nights. For younger plants and seedlings, dilute 1 to 20 with water, and for container plants dilute 1 to 30 with water.

Don't worry about getting the exact strengths exactly right, it's just that urine is high in nitrogen and has a lot of mineral salts in it, so it can burn plants. These salts are a good reason to try to avoid applying urine directly to plant leaves; it's best to pour it out in the soil around plants.

Apply weekly to fast growing and large plants, less often to very young and slower growing plants.

Your whizzer is the one thing you don't need to remember to pack! There are no doubts about the effectiveness of urine as a near perfect, soluble fertilizer on your garden.

I'll leave it up to you and your imagination how you go about adding urine around your plants or whether or not your aim is good. High in nitrogen, urea contains more phosphorous and potassium than many of the fertilizers we buy at the store!

Look that ratio of 1 to 20 is hard to think about when considering your bladder and a container if it ain`t

DIG IN AND FERTILIZE!

marked and of sufficient volume to accommodate you unless it is give me a urine sample at the doc's and it seems you never have enough.

If you want to mix it mentally, a good ratio of urine to water would be 1:8. You can collect a cup of urine and pour it into 8 cups of water in a plastic bucket used outside for fertilizing plants.

Pour 2 cups around the perimeter of each SMALL plant. For MEDIUM plants add 4 cups and LARGE plants deserve a good 6 cups of your own personal home grown brew. Water with this soluble solution once a week or so water hydration supplies permitting. Not too much or you will have all leaves and no fruit.

FOREST FODDER

I think it is safe to say most bug out locations will have access to a bunch of leaves on the ground, they all work but here is a specific fertilizer recipe to help all you want-to-be bug out preppers out.

Oak leaves: Fill 1/3 of a five-gallon bucket with dry oak leaves and add water to the top of the bucket. Place the mixture in a sunny spot and let it steep in the sun preferably until the water takes on the color of iced tea (ideally for one week). If the entire wait seems to be too long then add boiling water to the leaves and use the solution once it is cold. Do not waste the left over oak leaves; use them to make a dandy mulch.

DIG IN AND FERTILIZE!

No trees? No problem in fact better fertilizer is made from weeds and other herbaceous plants.

WEEDS – You have literally got your own fertilizer growing under your own two feet! **Could be weeds are your ready made food garden also but we will get into that later.**

To just name a few of the many beneficial weeds you are likely to encounter are Nettles, comfrey, yellow dock, burdock, horsetail and chickweed make wonderful homemade fertilizer. There are several ways you can utilize green leafy matter to make your own brew or to help speed up your compost pile. Another thing to consider is if your weeds have not gone to flower you can cut them down and dry them in the sun to use as a mulch. Weeds are high in nitrogen.

Borage (starflower) is an herb but for some people they say it's a weed. It has many of the same nutritional properties as comfrey. It is also said to increase the flavor of tomatoes and repel horned caterpillars. What you do is dry the entire plant, root and all, and put it in your compost tumbler or pile.

Borage helps break everything down and gives the pile an extra dose of heat. A jump start as it were.

Some folks let the weeds soak for many days in a bucket of water. For an extended brew, get out the bucket and your bandana! The bandana you might find you need for your nose because this technique gets rather stinky!

DIG IN AND FERTILIZE!

I am not in any way a fan of fermented fertilizers but if you want to take the "putrid plunge" and figure stinking stuff like fresh manure is worth playing with, place a bunch of weed leaves and roots in a 5 gallon bucket. Weigh down the leaves with a brick to ensure the plant matter is covered and add water to cover.

Stir weekly and wait 3-5 weeks for the contents to get thick and gooey. Then use that fetid smelling goo, diluted 1:10 or more as a soil drench fertilizer. To make it even more convenient, you can use two buckets and make a hole in the bottom of the bucket that contains the plants.

The sludgy goo will seep through to the lower bucket. Remember that it is always best to apply the liquid fertilizer diluted – it should look like weak tea.

You can use any combination of herbaceous plants to create fertilizer, put them in a container, fill with water, and cover with a fairly air-tight lid.

Leave it for a few days to a couple of weeks or months, and you have an herbal tea. Especially consider that if you forget about it for awhile that if you leave it for long enough that the bad smell mostly will go away, the resulting brew will contain many nutrients and beneficial microbes from the plants.

GRASS CLIPPINGS – this material is beneficially rich in nitrogen, grass breaks down over time and enhances the soil. **Fill a 5 gallon bucket full of grass clippings.** You can even add weeds! Weeds soak up nutrients from the soil just as much as grass. Add water to the top of the bucket and let sit for a day or two. Dilute

DIG IN AND FERTILIZE!

your grass tea by mixing 1 cup of liquid grass into 10 cups of water. Apply to the base of plants using the same amounts as listed above in the urine recipe.

Keep in mind grass seed in the garden is not welcome and by the way if you ever try hay bale gardening and use wheat straw I can almost guarantee you will have a huge clump of wheat grass where it was sitting, so you may want that, I personally don't.

You don't have to spend hundreds of dollars buying fertilizer at the local gardening store. By using items around your house, you can make an effective vegetable fertilizer with little effort or money. Most ingredients used for homemade fertilizers are things you would normally throw into the trash or have on hand already.

Use your food scraps to grow healthy vegetables. Although plants will grow as long as they have soil, water and light, fertilizer can be used to help the plants grow faster and appear more vibrant. Store bought fertilizers contain chemicals that can burn the plants if not used properly.

It is much safer for the plants when you create a homemade fertilizer to use. This fertilizer should contain baking soda, which eliminates the growth of fungal diseases that will hinder the plant's growth. Backyard gardeners truly think that baking soda's anti-fungal properties are as good if not better than store bought chemicals.

DIG IN AND FERTILIZE!

Zucchini, tomatoes, potatoes, pumpkin, melons, cabbage, squash, flowers and even fruit trees can be killed or damaged by blight or powdery mildew.

How it works is powdery mildew is a fungus that will attack the immune system of a plant or it will enter a plant's most productive phase when fruit is just about ready to ripen.

If not treated in time, baking soda may not halt fungal attack plants but it will help to slow the advance of the disease and prevent its outbreak to other plants. Once you use baking soda in your garden, you'll always use baking soda.

Make a Spray to Prevent & Treat Powdery Mildew.

Powdery mildew can be a problem for many plants. Plants prone to damaging powdery mildew include cabbages, bergamot or bee balm plants, squash, zinnias, lilacs, mushrooms, tomato, etc.

Cucumber and Squashes are particularly susceptible to powdery mildew which can eventually affect the plants immune system and kill it off. Stressed plants also attract bugs out the wazoo.

There's nothing worse than watching your plant grow to maturity, bloom and fruit and powdery mildew kill it off. Just makes you sick to your stomach. A simple mixture of baking soda, water, and dish detergent can really save your cucumber crop or deter the mildew from even happening.

DIG IN AND FERTILIZE!

2. Sprinkle Baking Soda on Cabbages (and other Brassicas) to Thwart Caterpillars, Aphids, Ants, Silver Fish and Roaches and some beetles away. Put directly onto slugs to kill them. Caterpillars can wipe out an entire crop of cabbage within a few days. Aphids can multiply so fast that a cabbage can be unrecognizable.

Caterpillars are the worst garden offenders. Those cute and colorful worms are like punks in a mash pit. When your cabbage begins to look like Swiss cheese.. You know you have caterpillars and its time to break out the baking soda or other remedy.

Make a 50/50 combination of flour (don't matter if it is self rising etc.) and baking soda, and dust it all over whichever plants the cabbage worms are eating. The mixture is good for most vegetable plants particularly cabbage, broccoli, and kale plants which caterpillars love. They'll eat the combo while munching on the leaves and will die within a day or so. Repeat as necessary.

NOTE: The birds will enjoy the caterpillars for dinner!

3. Sweeping Baking Soda into Sidewalk Cracks Discourages Weeds

Simply pour or sweep a thick layer of baking soda into sidewalk and patio cracks. The baking soda will kill any small weeds that are already there, and prevent new ones from sprouting. No worries about most flowers being

DIG IN AND FERTILIZE!

affected by baking soda. Baking soda can also help your PH balance in your soil.

4. Kill Crabgrass – No Match For Baking Soda!

Crabgrass can take over a lawn. Once you begin to notice crabgrass in your lawn, garden beds, or sidewalk cracks, you can use baking soda to get rid of it for good. Simply wet down all that nasty crabgrass or weed then pour a thick dusting of baking soda on it. The crabgrass will start dying back in two to three days. Caution Jungle Jim! Be careful where you're applying the baking soda because, too much baking soda on grass will offset the PH balance and kill common grasses. Grass is different than flower or vegetable plants.

5. Tomato Sweetener - Sweeten your tomatoes by sprinkling baking soda onto the soil around the plants.

6. Rabbit Deterrent - Sprinkle baking soda around your garden to keep the rabbits from eating your herbs and veggies.

7. Control Post harvest Diseases on fruits. Baking soda is more effective when combined with yeast organisms that prevent diseases from growing than expensive chemicals.

8. **Clean Garden Tools** - Baking soda is the perfect abrasive to clean all of the gunk and organic build-up on your garden tools. What's good for your teeth surely is good for your garden tools.

9. Keep Seeds Dry - Keep an envelope, box, sachet, or what have you of baking soda inside of your seed box to

DIG IN AND FERTILIZE!

keep your seeds dry. Keep your precious seeds safe from humidity.

10. **Clean Nails & Cuticles -** All of us backyard gardeners have at least one thing in common and that's dirty fingernails and feet. For soft, clean nails without a trip to the manicurist, simply dip your hands and feet in a bowl of warm water mixed with baking soda. Baking soda is cheaper and easier to come by than Epsom salt.

*For clean and exfoliated feet and hands, scrub with baking soda and your favorite soap. This will leave nails and cuticles cleaner and softer than water alone. Baking soda is good for the entire body. Instead of buying expensive exfoliators or sugars, use baking soda and a dab of liquid soap or your favorite bar soap. You'll figure out how much is good for your body type. Be sure to moisturize afterwards. *Also works to even discolored armpit skin which is usually caused from deodorant or bacteria.

11. **Laundry / Stain Remover -** Ahh grass and soil stains. We all love them, right? Clean discolored or stained socks with baking soda. I tend to clean my socks separately in a bucket before I add them to the regular wash load. You can add ½ cup of baking soda to your wash load and I guarantee that it will boost your detergents cleaning and whitening power. Ring-around-the-collar and armpit stains be gone!

12. Clean Fruits and Vegetables - Add 2 tablespoons of baking soda and a drop of dish soap to one gallon of water to clean fruits and vegetables. Vinegar also

DIG IN AND FERTILIZE!

works for cleaning vegetables. Dunk vegetables in solution then double dip in clean water. Do this particularly when you are using body fluids and such for fertilizer if there is a doubt about you or others health.

13. Fertilizer - Take a gallon of warm water and mix 1 tsp. of each Epsom salt, baking powder, saltpeter and 1/2 teaspoon of ammonia. Use this as a fertilizer in your houseplants

14. PH level - Wet soil and take a small amount of baking soda and sprinkle onto soil, if it bubbles your soil is acidic with a PH level under 5.

15. Black Spots on Roses - Mix 1 Tbsp. of baking soda and 1 tsp. of dawn dishwashing soap in a gallon of warm water. Spray on roses every ten days to prevent and treat black spot disease.

16. Keep cut flowers fresh longer by adding a teaspoon baking soda to the water in the vase. I personally say just drop a half of an aspirin in them depending on volume.

17. Soak dried beans in a baking soda solution to make them more digestible. Less gas.

DIG IN AND FERTILIZE!

18. Rubber Gloves - Trouble getting on rubber gloves? Just sprinkle in some baking soda and they'll slip right on.

19. Baking Soda **kills moss** and slimy green / black stains on house or RV! Baking soda isn't harmful to the rest of your lawn and plants, but it will cause lawn moss to turn brown and die within a week. Sprinkle baking soda directly on the lawn moss, either right out of the container or out of a shaker. I like to make my own shaker by taking a small drill bit and make holes directly into the baking soda box. To speed up ridding lawn moss, mix baking soda and a couple of drops of vinegar with water. Baking soda mixed with either water or vinegar to make a thick paste will completely get rid of moss / fungal stains.

20. Flowers and planting pots - Coat clay and terra cotta pots with a thin layer of baking soda when transplanting plants but before adding the soil. This helps keep the dirt fresh and resistant to fungus. If you have **cut flowers**, dip them in a solution of baking soda and water to keep water clear and to lengthen cut flower's life. A pinch in your pickle jar of sun iced tea will also keep the water clear and keep the tea from getting milky. No worries, you won't taste a thing and a pinch is enough for a gallon and tasteless.

*21. Brighten and Whiten Toenails and Fingernails! Mix two parts baking soda and one part (2-1) hydrogen peroxide. Rub paste onto toe nails and fingernails. You're going to thank me for this tip. Once you try it. You'll use this tip at least once a month. Backyard gardeners are working with soil, vegetation, water, etc. all which can dull

DIG IN AND FERTILIZE!

or stain toe and fingernails.

Really rub in into your nails, underneath your nails and into the creases around your nails. You are going to be amazed! You're welcome :O)

*22. **Remove labels from garden pots and garden decorations -** There's nothing worse than buying a beautiful ceramic garden pot, pretty patio accessories or dishes for your next bar-b-que and you can't seem to remove that pesky price tag or manufactures label. Here's a homemade sticker remover that will save you money from having to buy a professional adhesive goo remover. Mix 1/3 cup baking soda and 2/3 cup of vegetable oil. It works every time. Give it a try.

Safe Organic Pesticide – Make a safe and organic pesticide spray that can kill insects harmful to plants, like aphids, while not harming beneficial insects.

- Mix 1 teaspoon of baking soda
- 1/3 cup of cooking oil

Measure out 2 teaspoons of the mix and add it to 1 cup of water. Add this water to your plant sprayer.

DYI Miracle Grow

Ingredients:

- 1 gallon of water
- 1 tbsp Epsom salt
- 1 tsp baking soda

DIG IN AND FERTILIZE!

- 1/2 tsp of Household ammonia

Mix all ingredients together and use once a month on your plants or every couple weeks in poor soil conditions.

Shannon's Homemade Monster Tomato Fertilizer recipe:

- 2-3 dozen crush egg shells
- 2 cups bone meal
- 1/2 cup Epsom salts
- 14 crushed aspirin (a natural rooting hormone!)

Instructions for up graded homemade vegetable fertilizer

- 1

Pour 1 gallon of hot water into a small bucket.

- 2

Add 1 teaspoon of baking soda and 1 tablespoon of Epsom salts to the hot water. Stir until both ingredients have dissolved.

DIG IN AND FERTILIZE!

3

Pour 1/2 cup of molasses and 1/4 teaspoon of ammonia in the bucket. Stir again to combine all of the ingredients.

- 4

Set the baking soda fertilizer aside until it cools to room temperature.

- 5

Pour 1 cup of the homemade baking soda fertilizer into the soil of each plant. Repeat monthly to encourage your plants to grow healthy and strong.

DIG IN AND FERTILIZE!

Neat way to add water to the garden or add heat to a winter garden.

Hydrogen Peroxide

Certainly hydrogen peroxide is handy and dandy in the home, from stopping tooth infections to wiping down surfaces, and 101 other uses.

In the garden, either as a general fertilizer, fungicide or weed killer, H2O2 would be quite expensive,

DIG IN AND FERTILIZE!

but you may be able to buy it more cheaply, or in bulk where you are.

A 3% concentrate solution is usually used for home or personal use, and the garden is the same. Higher concentrations can be dangerous and can burn skin and eyes. If you buy hydrogen peroxide at a stronger concentration such as 10% or more, remember to handle carefully when diluting with water before use.

Advocates of hydrogen peroxide for plant use, do so because it is a powerful oxidizer. As it combines with outside air and water it decomposes, freeing its oxygen elements. Thus it provides a supplement of oxygen to plants and aerates the soil.

Here are some ways to use Hydrogen Peroxide in the Garden

1. As a general fertilizer to enhance plant growth, use 1 teaspoon of 3% hydrogen peroxide to 1 cup of water or ½ cup h2o2 to 4 liters (1 gal).
2. Use as a foliar spray or soil soak to help produce strong, healthy roots.

Use to water newly sown seeds, or even to soak seeds in before planting.

Use this mixture when rooting cuttings, either in the water they soak in or in the soil they are in.

3. To deter and kill of mold, bacterial and fungal infections, double the above

DIG IN AND FERTILIZE!

concentration at least, ie: 2-3 teaspoons per cup of water, or 1¼ cup per 4 liters (1 gal).

Spray on top and under leaves to combat blight, downy mildew and other fungal spores. Water in around plants to treat collar and root rot, and soil born pests.

To stop infections, paint or spray on pruning cuts. Dip secateurs in mixture to sterilize them.

4. To use as a weed killer, apply neat strength. If you can buy a stronger concentration than 3%, say 10%, this is more effective for killing weeds.

Pet and Human Hair

Pet (cat, dog, ferret, guinea pig, etc) and human hair is a fantastic material for using in tomato fertilizer.

Hair contains keratin which is a valuable protein. Hair contains good levels of nitrogen, sulfate and small traces of other minerals. Hair takes time to break down, which makes it a slow release fertilizer

Adding Crumbled Eggshells

Why: Eggshells are rich in calcium. A calcium deficiency in tomatoes will cause blossom rot, that ugly brown patch on the bottom of the fruit.

DIG IN AND FERTILIZE!

How: Place crumbled eggshells in the bottom of your planting hole, or dig them into the soil around the base of your tomato plant.

Bonus: If slugs plague your garden, place crumbled eggshells around the bottom of plants. The shards will cut the slimy pests.

Compost Tea:

Get a clean glass jar. Add water to the jar. Keep it on your counter. Whenever you use eggs, crunch up the shells and put them into the jar. The same goes for coffee ground. Put them into the jar. Once you have quite a bit of this mix, add more water, shake and let it sit for a while.

It will need to sit for quite a while and you will need to shake it every day. Do not keep the jar in direct sunlight.

Epsom Salt Fertilizer: Did you know that <u>Epsom salt</u> is a common fertilizer that can be used in your yard and garden? Right on the bag it says that you can sprinkle 2 tbsp. of <u>Epsom</u> salts around the base of tomatoes, roses, evergreens, azaleas, rhododendrons, and trees. It is also great for fertilizing indoor plants.

Use in Place of:

DIG IN AND FERTILIZE!

Houseplant food
Vegetable fertilizer
Rose plant food

What You Need:

- 1 Tablespoon Epsom Salt
- 1 gallon water
- A watering can

What You Do:

1. Combine the Epsom salt and water.
2. Use the solution to water your plants.
3. Repeat once a month.

Why This Works:

Epsom salt is made up of magnesium and sulfate – both vital plant nutrients. Some magnesium-loving plants to try it on: houseplants, roses, peppers, tomatoes and potatoes.

Fireplace Ash Fertilizer

Use in Place of:

Garden fertilizer
Lime

What You Need:

- Fireplace ash

What You Do:

DIG IN AND FERTILIZE!

1. Sprinkle your fireplace ash over your garden beds, and work into the soil.

Note: Fireplace ash should not be used if your soil is alkaline, or be used much around acid-loving plants.

Why This Works:

Fireplace ash is rich in potassium and calcium carbonate.

Vinegar Fertilizer

Use in Place of:

Houseplant fertilizer
Rose plant food

What You Need:

- 1 Tablespoon white vinegar
- 1 gallon water
- A watering can

What You Do:

1. Combine the white vinegar and water.
2. Use the solution to water your plants.
3. Repeat every three months.

Why This Works:

The acetic acid in vinegar works to increase the acidity of the soil – just the thing for acid-loving plants.

DIG IN AND FERTILIZE!

Weed compost tea:

Similar to the coffee/tea version but you use weeds. Don't use any weeds that have been treated with herbicide. Place the weeds in a jar with rain water. Cover and place in the sun. It will smell really foul, but in a week you will have your "weed compost tea." This mixture is e far more effective than miracle grow and will last the entire season in the ground.

One of the fundamental principles of organic gardening is to "feed the soil, not the plant." The idea behind this concept is that if you start with healthy soil in the first place, you won't need a lot of additional fertilizers. That's good advice, but sometimes even Mother Nature appreciates a little boost. Organic liquid fertilizers and teas are good options, because they can provide plants with nutrients in a readily available form. Here's all you need to know to make your own.

Fertilizer & Tea-Making Methods

Inverted Plastic Bottle (with cap)

This passive method works well for making small quantities of very concentrated liquid fertilizer from plant leaves. Stuff the bottle full of leaves (see appropriate plants below) and top them off with a sprinkle of water. Drill a tiny hole into the bottle cap and screw it back onto the bottle. This is where the concentrate will drip out. Place the bottle, cap-side-down, over a small container to collect the dripping concentrate. After 2 to 3 weeks (maybe sooner) a dark liquid will drip out. Dilute the concentrate with 10 to 15 parts water.

DIG IN AND FERTILIZE!

Bucket & Strainer

This is another passive technique for making fertilizer tea. Fill an aged burlap sack or old nylon stocking filled with your fertilizer source and immerse it in a 5 gallon bucket filled with water. Add 1 ounce of unsulfured molasses (to provide a food for beneficial organisms). Cover the bucket and allow it to steep for the directed amount of time. When finished, strain off the solids by carefully lifting out the burlap or nylon stocking. The solids can be returned to the compost pile or worked into the soil. Fermenting times: plants = 2 - 4 weeks; manure or prepared fish emulsion paste* = 1-2 weeks.

Bubble & Brew

Use a bucket and a small aquarium pump to speed up the fermentation process. Using 3 ft. of aquarium hose, attach one end to a small aerating pump and place the other end at the bottom of a five gallon bucket. For more bubbles, use a gang valve (available at aquarium supply stores) to divide the airflow from the hose into three separate streams. All three hose streams should reach the bottom of the bucket. Fill the bucket with approximately 1 gallon of your compost, making sure that the ends of the hose are covered. Fill the rest of the bucket to within 6 inches of the top with water and add 1 ounce of unsulfured molasses (to provide a food for beneficial organisms). Bubble and brew for liquid fertilizer in 2-3 days. The brew will have a yeasty smell or a foamy top layer when finished.

Common Organic Liquid Fertilizers

Liquid Manures:

These are commonly made from cow, horse, sheep or poultry manure. Another great and often overlooked source of "barnyard" manure is the rabbit. Rabbit droppings contain one of the highest concentrations of nitrogen. They are small and compact and they don't have the pronounced smell that most other animal manures have.

To Make Your Own: Use the bucket and strainer method or the bubble and brew method. Strain out solids and dilute 1:1 with water before applying to soil or as a foliar spray.

Fish Emulsion:
This fertilizer is made up of the waste by-products of the fishing industry, namely the fish meal trade or the fish canning industry. Fish emulsion is high in nitrogen and contains readily soluble phosphorus and potassium. It should not be confused with fish meal, which is typically used as a soil conditioner and food for soil microorganisms.

To Make Your Own: If you are using fresh fish, you need to compost it separately in a 5 gallon bucket before you make it into liquid fertilizer. Add fresh fish and fill at least half of the bucket with browns like leaves, straw or sawdust. Add an ounce or more of unsulfured molasses to reduce odors and encourage beneficial microbials. Cover and let rot for 1-2 weeks, opening the bucket to stir and allow for air circulation every 2 days. Once the fish is well rotted, use one of the methods above to make liquid fertilizer. Seaweed can be added in at this time.

Seaweed:
Because of its low nitrogen and phosphorus levels, seaweed is often combined with fish emulsion before

DIG IN AND FERTILIZE!

being applied as a fertilizer. By itself, seaweed is a rich source of potassium, but it is considered more of a growth stimulant than a fertilizer. It contains several important trace elements, specific carbohydrates and growth hormones that benefits plants. One way to use seaweed extract effectively is to soak seeds in it for 24 hours prior to planting. It can also be applied to the soil around young plants to increase root growth or sprayed on their foliage to increase chlorophyll content while discouraging sap-sucking insects.

To Make Your Own: Collect enough seaweed to fill a plastic trash can (or any container of your choice) half way to the top. The plant tissues will naturally contain some salt, but it's a good idea to rinse any excess salt off of the surface of the seaweed before putting it into the barrel. Top off the container with water and allow it to stand for 2 to 3 months. As the seaweed decomposes, the water will turn brown. Chopping it up into small pieces will help it decompose faster. The resulting liquid will be highly concentrated and should be diluted with water (1:1) before being applied. Dried seaweed is useful for making up smaller quantities or if you don't have access to fresh plants.

Rock Phosphate:
Phosphorus is the essential nutrient primarily responsible for healthy root development and fruit and flower production.

To Make Your Own: In order for it to remain suspended in liquid form, rock phosphate needs to be pulverized into a fine powder. Since most people lack the necessary tools to do this effectively, buying it is more practical for most gardeners.

DIG IN AND FERTILIZE!

Plant Extracts:
Comfrey, chamomile, yarrow and nettle all serve double duty in the garden. Not only can they be used for their herbal properties, but they also make wonderful all-purpose fertilizers that you can grow and harvest as needed.

To Make You're Own: Use any of the above methods to steep leaves into a concentrate or liquid fertilizer tea.

How Much & How Often
Like any fertilizers, organic liquid fertilizers should not be a substitute for healthy soil. Don't overdo it. Use them as a short-term solution when conditions warrant it, such as container gardening or when weather delays transplanting. Liquid fertilizers are concentrated and can burn a plant's leaves and roots. Always dilute them with water before applying them. Plant concentrates can be stored in a cool, dry place for a few months, but manure and fish-based fertilizers should be used immediately. Container plants can be fed 2-3 times per week and houseplants every other week during the active growing season.

Soil Drenches: Use liquid fertilizers to help build up microbial activity in soil and supply NPK to the plant's root system.

You might try Epsom salts for magnesium. If it's nitrogen you are lacking, here is a country solution, literally. Make a 10:1 solution of water to urine. Water with this once a week or so. Not too much or you will have all leaves and no fruit!

DIG IN AND FERTILIZE!

Foliar Feeds: When plants that have suffered serious root damage, or you need a quick fix of soluble trace elements, apply liquid fertilizer as a foliar spray to plant leaves.

Make Herb Tea Fertilizer

Did you know you can make liquid fertilizer for your plants using other plants?

1. Fill up a bucket, large jar, or other container with the leaves, stems and flowers of pruned herbs. Pack them in tightly. There is no need to remove the entire plant. Just cut it back and you will be able to make another batch next month.
2. Pour in water, filling your container to the top.
3. Let the whole mess sit for a day. Put it in the sun to speed things up.
4. Strain out the herbs and fill up a spray bottle or watering can with the concoction.

You can spray the leaves of your plants with this mix as a foliar fertilizer, or just pour it onto the soil.

Herbs to Try:

Comfrey - High in magnesium, phosphorous, and potassium.
Stinging Nettle - Contains magnesium, sulphur, and iron.
Horsetail - Loaded with silica, a nutrient that makes plants strong.

Molasses Fertilizer

DIG IN AND FERTILIZE!

Molasses has a 1-0-5 NPK ratio while also containing potash, sulfur, and trace minerals. Molasses for years has been used as a nutritional soil amendment, a carbohydrate source to feed and stimulate organisms, and a chelating agent.

Molasses can come in 2 forms. One is in liquid form that can simply be bought at the store. The second is dry molasses which is molasses sprayed on grain residue and dried. But regardless of which form you use blackstrap molasses is the type of molasses with the highest level of sulfur, iron, and micronutrients, which is excellent for man and soil.

Molasses as a fertilizer works by "feeding the soil not the plant." It provides carbohydrates to the "micro-herd" that works with plant roots to digest and absorb nutrients. Also the micronutrients help the "micro-herd" to use trace minerals as catalysts to make enzymes that create biochemical transformations in other words the "micro-herd" breaks down organic fertilizer and "feeds" it to the plants. Molasses also works as a chelating agent, which is to simply say that a "magical" substance converts one chemical nutrient that plants or animals cannot use into one that can be used.

Molasses is a versatile product that can work as a plant food or as an additive to improve a fertilizer mix or tea. Dry molasses can be used in a fertilizer mix while liquid molasses or blackstrap molasses can be used alone or as part of both sprays and soil drenches.

Dry molasses from the seed and feed store can be mixed into your own personal soil potting mix at 1 cup of dried molasses per 10 gallons of soil mix. It can also be

DIG IN AND FERTILIZE!

mixed with water, compost tea, or manure tea. This can be mixed at 1 tablespoon per gallon of water. The easiest and cheapest form of dry molasses comes from horse feed.

Blackstrap molasses are great for watering and foliar feeding when mixed with organic teas. A simple recipe for Manure Tea Sweetened with Blackstrap Molasses and Alfalfa Meal Tea Sweetened with Blackstrap Molasses is below.

Manure Tea Sweetened with Blackstrap Molasses

Ingredients

- 1 gallon of Water
- 1 Tablespoon of Guano (Or 1 and a ½ TBS composted cow manure
- 1 teaspoon Blackstrap Molasses

Place guano in a lady's nylon and tie off. Put in water and soak for 24 hours. Stir frequently. Water as usual and place used guano or cow manure in compost. Use as you would a normal liquid fertilizer.

Alfalfa Meal Tea Sweetened with Blackstrap Molasses

Ingredients

- 4 gallons of Water
- 1 cup of fine Alfalfa Meal
- 1 tablespoon Blackstrap Molasses

DIG IN AND FERTILIZE!

This tea is great as a foliar feed, which for the novice simply means spraying the leaves where nutrients are absorbed through the plant's pores.

Hot pepper is a natural deterrent for many types of pests in the garden. To make your own homemade pepper spray, combine 6-10 hot peppers and two cups of water in a blender and blend on high speed for 1-2 minutes, pour the liquid into a storage container to sit overnight and then strain out the pulp. Add this liquid to one quart of water in a sprayer, and spray your plants liberally every week or after each rain.

Tomato leaves are packed with alkaloids, which can be an effective repellant for aphids, corn earworms and Diamondback moths. Several good gardening sites on the internet recommend soaking 1 to 2 cups of chopped or mashed tomato leaves in two cups of water overnight, straining it through a fine mesh and adding two more cups of water before spraying it on the plants in your garden. Keep this mixture away from pets, as tomato leaves can be toxic.

DIG IN AND FERTILIZE!

CASTILE SOAP

Is there anything castile soap can't do? The gentle vegetable oil-based soap makes a gentle and effective insecticidal spray for the garden. Dr. Bronner's, the company that makes the most prevalent brand of castile soap, recommends filling a spray bottle with water and adding a tablespoon of either unscented or peppermint castile soap and a pinch of either cayenne pepper, cinnamon or powdered garlic. This mixture will kill aphids, mealybugs, whiteflies and spider mites.

Enzymatically Digested Hydrolized Liquid Fish

Standard fish emulsion products add nitrogen and micronutrients, but they have a strong smell. Spend a bit more money on enzymatically digested hydrolized fish liquid, available at nurseries and garden centers, instead. These products don't smell and they offer more nutrients than fish emulsions. Combine 5 tablespoons liquid fish with 1 gallon of water. Apply the liquid fish as a foliar spray or water the ground directly.

We've got this gift of love, but love is like a precious plant. You can't just accept it and leave it in the cupboard or just think it's going to get on by itself. You've got to keep watering it. You've got to really look after it and nurture it.
John Lennon

3

JOIN THE BUCKET BRIGADE

Ok in the last chapter I think you have hopefully learned just enough about fertilizers to give you an extra edge trying to grow those survival seeds you got stuck in your bug out bag. Lots of formulas and dry reading for some but it got you to the point where I can tell you a story that will help you remember what all it entails to actually put into practice all these tid bits of info I am telling you.

You should be able by now to understand why what few items I throw in my (BGB) bug out garden bucket are worth their weight and nominal expense. I also gave you a bit of advice on using nothing but what you can find on site but why not carry some extra stuff with you if you plan on raising a survival or victory garden?

So get yourself a bucket suitable for a bug out and put in it these items.

(1) box of Epsom Salt
(2) Box of Baking Soda
(3) Bottle of Household Ammonia
(4) Bottle of Castiile soap or dish washing liquid
(5) A couple quality empty spray bottles
(6) This book inside a plastic bag
(7) 2 lbs of Contender beans
(8) Entrenching tool

Carry your survival seeds in your pack where they will remain safe in case any of those liquids spring a leak.

That's it! Now then, you might want to add salt peter (Potassium Nitrate) from drug store, peroxide, hot sauce, and molasses, aspirin (Scientists have found that aspirin multiplies a plant's natural defenses against deadly viruses, bacteria, fungi and actually repels insects! For using this miracle drug in your flower beds and vegetable garden, mix 1 ½ uncoated, finely ground aspirin tablets and 2 TBS. baby shampoo in 2 gallons of water. Use a handheld sprayer and spray your plants every 3 weeks during the growing season.)

This do it yourself fertilizing kit will last you several seasons and if you are a practicing gardener be sure just to treat it as a backup prep and don't get into it unless truly necessary.

Now then you arrive on your impromptu relocation site and have picked you out a likely place to put in your bug out garden. (We will get into how to pick that out later.) You grab your handy dandy entrenching tool and fold it into an L shape and proceed to start digging like a dog with both hands on the shovel, feet splayed and bent at the waist.

This task is not as labor intensive as it sounds and you can make great headway in a short period of time. Try it one day, you will like the results and it's easier to break ground or clear out weeds this way. Hey speaking of weeds, did you survey the area well for edible weeds?

Don't be digging up your best dandelion patch just because you think its ascetically pleasing to put your garden there. Hell if they are already growing you are already blessed with an edible source for eating so think twice about what it is you're taking out of the equation. Ok so now your back to digging along and learning the rhythm of the task while keeping in mind that all this land clearing is also creating a whole lot of food and fertilizer. You might as well make up your mind now to get used to eating weeds for awhile to extend your rations while you are waiting on your veggies to grow. A little bit goes a long way. Wild plants are very potent so it is best to start by ingesting small amounts. Begin by nibbling a taste of a common wild edible plant and slowly introduce it to your body and taste buds.

Set aside what you know to be wild edibles and plan on having a small portion for dinner tonight, the rest that you don't use will get buried in your newly but lightly turned soil. Don't go down more than about 3-4 inches. The weeds you pull or gather up in the process here and there use to make you up some compost tea for fertilizer.

While you are busy digging holes and raising beds, think about where you're going to put your latrine and don't forget to save your pee when you can for fertilizer.

Do you have empty bottles or jars for that? Yea everything you need but containers to put it in is out here at the bug out location so plan accordingly. Don't just be grabbing up all that green matter with your bare hands either, use the tool or put on work gloves. Now is not the time to get a weird rash or a thorn in your finger.

OK what we are going to create is a raised bed garden with out the wooden walls. Raised rows are very similar to raised beds – with a few minor cost saving changes. One, we do not use any edging, boards, stone, etc. to keep our beds in place. Not that it's inherently bad to do so – it just adds cost and maintenance issues in a normal garden that are not needed and in a bug out situation most likely these materials will not be available. For many of us just starting out in our new house or trailer in the country thinking about going to the expense of building traditional raised beds is a huge obstacle.

Basically you are making rows and walking paths by taking the dirt out of the paths and throwing it up to the left and right to raise the rows. After the ground is initially broken up, a square point shovel makes this task so much easier but it can still be done quite handily with an entrenching tool if it's all you got.

If you have room to bring your gardening tools with you on your bug out then by all means do so. I am just showing you the minimalist approach shy of a fire hardened digging stick. You can build "Raised Rows" (also know as wide-row gardening) to achieve many of the benefits of Raised Beds. In essence, raised rows are raised beds without a "container". Raised Rows demand the least amount of materials but are more labor-intensive

Look at what you're digging in; if you have a lot of clay in your soil the walk ways will hold water after a heavy rain which can be a good thing. Also notice where the top soil line is. You don't want to dig too deep, the idea is to get as much top soil on the row as you can and not bury it under all that less promising earth found underneath. Maybe 3 inches max. Be thinking about researching no till gardening. When you have the first layer roughly busted up throw your commercial fertilizer out if you have any and make sure it's somewhat evenly spread. Make your walkways by alternately throwing the dirt from them to the right and left. Pathway should be about three entrenching tools wide or two square point shovel fulls.

Tamp down the sides hard and lightly tamp down the top of your rows. You're ready to plant. If you're not using commercial fertilizer then apply one of your homemade concoctions to the rows before you plant. You

are now bug out gardening.

Garden layout diagram: 15' feet wide by 10' feet, with alternating Growing Rows (16" to 18" wide) and 20" to 24" wide walking rows.

Improve the soil, the position and the area time permitting. Put leaves in the walkways as mulch. As this biomass breaks down they will improve the soil and attract earthworms. This is one way you can also trench compost and when it's time for a winter garden or next season move one row over and keep shifting rows back and forth as you are improving the soil. If there are non invasive weeds in the paths leave them be and step around or turn them into pot herbs as needed for control and healthy benefits.

What is trench composting? You dig a trench (we're using the word "trench" loosely here; it doesn't matter what shape your hole is) approximately twelve inches deep, add roughly four to six inches of compostable materials, such as kitchen scraps, spent garden plants, prunings, thinnings, and weeds, and bury it with the soil you dug out of the trench.

.

The next step is…..well, there is no next step. Thing is you wont be adding any dirt this season because you used it to make your raised rows. It will make sense to you soon but don't worry about it for now and just consider whatever it is you add to your walk ways as mulch.

Learn for yourself something about companion planting, there are whole books written on the subject, if you know nothing about it don't fret, observe. You will notice sometimes bugs are busy munching one kind of weed in your garden versus your beans? You ever notice some plants mysteriously produce more or are healthier in the presence of another? Well that's it! Next go round encourage those types of conditions artificially by adding or subtracting things. Some plants don't like growing together like onions and strawberries where as carrots love tomatoes.

For this example I will guide you through setting up a 10' x 15' raised row bed garden area. Obviously, you can make your beds any size you wanted to by following the same principles and methods; however, a 10' x 15' set up will give the average family plenty of fresh vegetables throughout the growing season.

One assumption you can make in building a homestead garden versus a bug out garden is starting your raised row beds out right with a pick up load or two of additional topsoil and composted manure.

You certainly don't have to take this step especially if you are short on cash or have access to your own topsoil or compost mix at your disposal.

How To Build Your Raised Row Beds Gardens:
Once you have found the best available area on your farmstead or if you can prepare your bug out location– you can do a little work now that will help you come spring.

Here is all you need to get started:
1 to 2 bales of straw (or if you have them available for free – a few big bags of shredded leaves that you generally can get by driving around a neighborhood in the city in the fall)
1 sheet of black plastic big enough to cover an area 10' x 15'
4 or 5 rocks, cement blocks or spare 2 x 4's to hold down the plastic

Spread a sheet of heavy duty black plastic over the entire 10 x 15 area to help kill all the grass and weeds off of your future garden plot and you will have an easy no till garden to rock and roll on planting come spring.

Step 1 – Preparing The Space

Start out by spreading out the straw or shredded leaves over the entire 10' x 15' area. It should be at least a 3 to 4" thick layer. Now take your black plastic sheet, lay it on top of your layer of straw or leaves to completely cover the area.

This method will serve to eliminate almost all of the grass that now occupies the area you have chosen and keeps you from having to dig at all to get your space ready. After you have covered it up, secure the plastic down with your rocks, bricks, or whatever you can use to ensure it won't fly up during the winter and early spring. When complete, head inside and work on your preps as you enjoy the winter! You can also use this method in the early spring; just make sure to give the plastic a few weeks at minimum to kill off most of the grass underneath.

Step 2 – Building Your First Beds In The Spring
Here is all you need:
2 to 3 Bales Of Straw
2 Cubic Yards Of Topsoil Or Growers Mix

The Row Layout for a 10 x 15 Raised Row Garden

You can probably complete this next task in less than a half a day. In early spring, a few weeks before your ready to set in the first of your plants or seeds it is time to build the beds. Take off the rocks and plastic, and what you should hopefully find is some slightly decomposed leaves or straw. Most, if not all of the grass or growth that was underneath will have died off. Don't start raking or moving any of it because it's the start of your raised row beds

Start out by taking the straw (or you can use shredded leaves if you have available), and spread out a pile about 18" wide x 6" high the entire length on the edge of the 10' run. If you use straw then make sure to break it apart as you loosely spread it out while being careful not to leave it in matted clumps. If you use leaves make shredded ones are best, like ones run over by a lawnmower. Measure off about 22 to 24" of space for your walking row and make another pile 18" wide x 5" high x 10' long just like your first row. Continue doing so until you have made 5 rows, 18" wide – each the length of the 10' row. You will have two rows on the outer edge – and three rows in between. The 22 to 24" space in between will become your walking and picking rows.

Good Topsoil and Manure Mix is the one purchase that can pay for itself quickly and get your garden off to a quick and easy start

Step 3 – Adding Soil To Your Beds

About two cubic yards should be all you need for a 10 x 15 garden – and can fit easily in the back of a pick up truck. If you don't have access to a truck – they will usually deliver for an additional fee. Yes, it will cost a little here to get the garden up and running – but remember, this is a ONE-TIME only expense. Trust me that the vegetables you grow will easily pay for themselves in year 1! A couple of things to make sure of if you purchase: 1) Make sure your buying a good garden soil – and not fill dirt – and 2) Make sure its pulverized – it will make spreading out your soil a snap.

Once you have your straw base in place for your rows – you can shovel on about 5" to 6" of topsoil on top of the straw. You can smooth it all out with a rake when you're done to leave nice, smooth, raised rows.

Spread about 6 to 8" of soil over the top of each 18" wide straw planting rows. The goal here is not to make huge mounds, you just to want to cover the straw or leaves. It will just slightly raise the soil in the working beds from your walking rows. Don't worry if you see some straw peeking through, that is fine, its okay! Just scallop or grade your beds slightly down from their center height of 6 to 8" in the middle.

Once you're raised rows are built, take more of the straw and spread out a thick layer (about 6") in between the raised row beds. Newspaper or cardboard also works. This will help choke out any weeds, by not allowing any bare ground to be exposed for weed seeds to be blown into your walking spaces. It will mat down after a few times of walking on it – so be generous – the more you apply to the rows will mean the fewer weeds you will have to deal with later.

NOW YOU'RE READY TO PLANT!

This raised bed or row garden system you have created is very efficient. The soil gets warmer quicker for earlier planting; it tends to hold water better and once established is cleaner than just flat row cropping.

Get you a scuffle or stirrup hoe 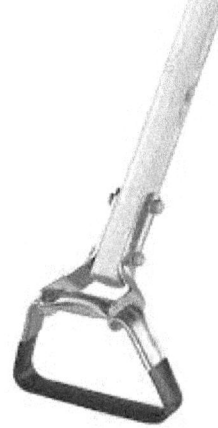 to weed with they are huge labor and time savers. An older version Swoe is my preference . Maybe you will get lucky and find an antique one like mine but I haven't seen any others but this one that was passed down to me and was manufactured brought back from England.

Join The Bucket Brigade

Join The Bucket Brigade

If you wait until your seeds get tall enough to distinguish them from the weeds all you have to do is an occasional leisurely pass or two with one of these to keep your garden pretty clean. Don't wait until you need one of those old fashion kind of hoes to get out there and chop weeds with, even if you do wait that long, a swoe is still much easier to work.

Direct seeding as I have suggested is hit or miss depending on the germination rate of your seeds, the conditions etc and first good rainfall will put many seeds too deep or washed away so plan on losses and reseeding some things after 14 days. I always have to go out first rain to push down beans that have somehow floated to the surface but after that everything seems to settle fine on its own.

I have put in acres by my own two hands and back with the above method over a span of several days with good results. Of course my best results came after spreading manure and going totally organic but we are talking time and money in this situation. I also had somebody disc my soil the first go round for that big of an area but that was a kind neighbor needing a few bucks and another venture. After that it was a few years of hand only until I could afford a tiller. The No-Till method of planting crops is used with much success by commercial farmers. There is no reason a similar method can't work for the backyard gardener as well.

As the soil settles, the beds will wind up being 6 to 8 inches high. Rake the soil smooth so the top of the bed is flat and the sides are a long, curved slope. When the first bed is finished, stake out the next 3-foot strip, allowing 12 to 18

Many folks make their gardens with very wide rows like the picture above for increased yields and production. This is too labor intensive with just a entrenching tool or throwing up a quick bug out garden without a tiller or a bunch of pick and shovel hand work

Determining bed widths

The length of the beds is not as important as the width. Plants in the center should be easily accessible from either side. That dictates a maximum width of 4 feet. In a 5- or 6-foot-wide bed, the center would be hard to reach without stepping on the bed. Vary your beds to be between 2 and 4 feet wide and as long as necessary.

Join The Bucket Brigade

Vegetables planted in beds should be set or sown so that each plant has just enough space to spread to its mature size (imagine that space as a circle) before touching the leaves of its neighbors. This arrangement is very space efficient and effectively smothers weeds. As the vegetables leaf out, the ground underneath is shaded, discouraging weed growth.

Thickly-planted beds need weeding only when the vegetables are seedlings. If an errant weed should push up above the mature vegetables, it's easy to pull out of the loose soil. Any weeds that sprout on the slanted side banks are easily uprooted with an occasional raking. Five minutes of hoeing takes care of any weeds that pop up in a walkway.

Raised beds save resources

Before converting to raised beds, you spread fertilizer over the entire garden. The paths between the vegetables, will take 60 to 70 percent of your garden space, and will also take 60 to 70 percent of fertilizer. The fertilized paths encourage weeds to grow faster and taller. Now fertilizer goes only on the beds-and not on the walkways. The same is true of water and mulch. Everything is used more efficiently in the raised-bed layout.

Make one row of your garden

"It's for people who can't afford to go buy bags and bags of potting soil,"

A Keyhole garden is a small organic vegetable patch which can efficiently provide plenty of food for your family. This design is typically used in Africa due to its water efficiency and reduces waste by incorporating a central composter to provide nutrients.

To forget how to dig the earth and to tend the soil is to forget ourselves. ~Mahatma Gandhi

Have you ever heard of a garden that waters and fertilizes itself? Keyhole garden A **keyhole garden** (so-called because of its shape) is a round raised garden, supported with stones

Is your backyard too hot and dry to cultivate the vegetables you have only dreamed of? Keyhole gardens were developed for the sole purpose of maximum crop output in the hottest and driest of conditions. Their low cost, low maintenance and versatility make them a desirable gardening option for your yard and for gardening across the globe.

A keyhole garden (so-called because of its shape) is a round raised garden, supported with stones. Keyhole gardens are built in places where it is difficult to build normal gardens (rocky areas, shallow arid/or compacted soils, etc), near the entrance of dwellings to facilitate their watering with household waste water. Keyhole gardens are made with low-cost locally available materials. The production of a keyhole garden can be enough to feed a family of 8 persons. Such gardens can produce food all year round even under harsh temperatures and can support the production of at least 5 varieties of vegetables at a time - thus supporting dietary diversity. Compared to regular vegetable gardens, keyhole gardens require less labor (ideal for elderly, children or sick persons), less water and no costly fertilizers or pesticides.

They act like an organic recycling tank, using your food and garden waste as fuel to grow vegetables! Crop rotation and growing of insect-repellent plants are important to balance nutrient demands, fight insects and plant diseases, and deter weeds.

Benefits of the Keyhole Garden

Soil enrichment
• The layers of organic materials decompose over time, adding nutrients to the soil.
• The central composting basket continuously replenishes the soil.

Moisture retention
• The layers soak up moisture, so the garden requires less water to remain moist.

Year-round vegetable production
• The stones of the keyhole garden wall absorb heat from the sun, protecting crops from cold winter temperatures.

Labor saving technology
• The soil re-nourishment and moisture retention reduce the amount of time required to maintain the garden.
• The garden shape makes it more accessible to sick or elderly gardeners.

Low-cost design
• All construction materials should be readily available (at

no cost) to gardeners.
• Gardeners might need to purchase seeds for planting, however.

Steps in Construction of a Keyhole Garden

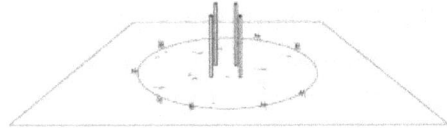

• A circle about 6 1/2 feet across is cleared.
• Four corner posts are secured into the ground.

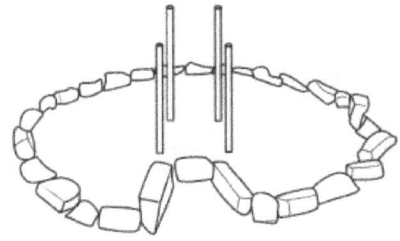

• The outline of the garden is marked with stones.
• The outline dips inwards at the center.

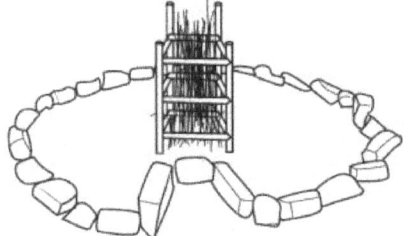

• The basket is encircled with rope and lined with thatching grass to allow water that is poured into the basket to flow into the garden soil.

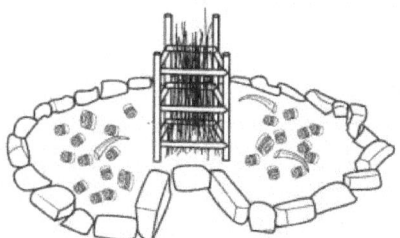

- The first layer of the garden is iron scraps such as empty food and beverage cans, aloe leaves, dry animal bones, broken clay pots, which can be substituted with fist-size stones
- These materials provide minerals to the soil as well as drainage in heavy rains.

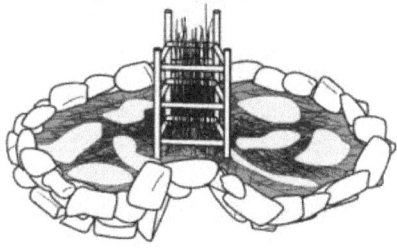

- The first layer is covered with soil that gives nutrients, thatching grass that retains moisture, and wood ash that provides potassium.
- Every layer should slope downwards from the basket so water can flow properly into the soil.
- Soil is added on top of the wood ash.

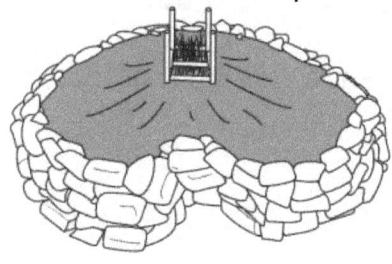

- Soil is added on top of the wood ash.
- A thick layer of mixed soil and dry manure is added on top. Using wet manure will kill young seedlings
- Add stones to the garden walls as the layers grow taller.

- Seeds are planted according to the season.
- During the winter, protect plants from the cold with thatching grass or old carpet. During the day, plants should be uncovered so they receive sunlight.

Planting Keyhole Garden

Space, soil nutrients, and pest management are key considerations in planning your garden. Companion planting is planting different kinds of crops together in the same garden in order to best satisfy those needs. Different methods include planting leafy crops next to root vegetables or planting pest-resistant vegetables (like onion or garlic) next to regular crops. To best ensure that your garden will
stay fertile and resist pests, plant a minimum of four vegetable types.

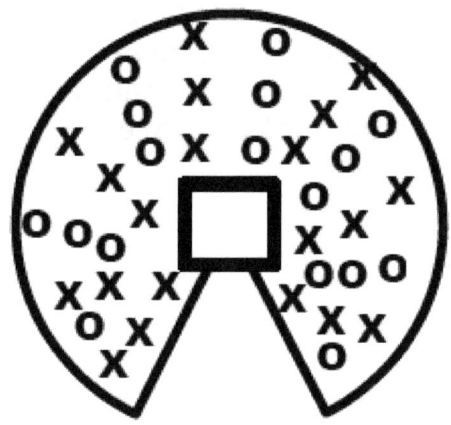

One idea for companion planting.
X: leafy plants
O: root plants

Preferred Crops For Keyhole Gardens

Root Crops

- Carrot
- Onion
- Beetroot
- Radish
- Turnips
- Garlic

Leafy Crops

- Spinach
- Swiss chard
- Lettuce
- Rape
- Mustard spinach
- Herbs

Crops *NOT* Recommended For Keyhole Gardens But I plant Them in Mine Anyway and have good luck, there are just easier ways to grow them and spreading plants take up a lot of space.

- Tomatoes
- Cabbage
- Peppers
- Eggplant
- Chilies
- Maize
- Peas
- Beans
- Potatoes
- Squash

Maintenance of the Keyhole Garden

Watering

- The garden should be watered regularly so that the garden soil is moist.
- Clean water is used on the topsoil.
- Water from washing hands, laundry, or dishes is poured into the basket. The thatch and the composting in the basket will clean the water.

Soil

- Dry manure and topsoil should be replenished in the garden so that it does not become sapped of its fertility.

Basket

- Uncooked vegetable scraps, dry manure, eggshells, and compost are added to the basket. These replenish the soil.
- The basket will decompose within 1 or 2 years and should be replaced.
- The garden wall near the basket can be pulled away, allowing gardeners to remove the old basket and replace it.

Garden construction

- Over time, the garden may lose its nutrients, and vegetables stop growing well. You then need to rebuild the garden. This is usually done every 4–5 years.

Why would I bother building one of these?

The ultimate answer, apart from the accessibility features mentioned earlier, is the efficient use of space. Consider creating a square, raised garden bed that you could access from every angle. It could only be 1m x 1m (3.3ft x 3.3ft) but would take up a space measuring 2m x 2m for access. Therefore, this one garden bed would require 4sq. meters but only provide 1sq. m of gardening plot. The arable portion of this plot is only 25%.

A keyhole garden, on the other hand – with the measurements quoted earlier, would take up an area totaling 9 sq.ms and provide a plot size of 5.78 sq.ms. The arable portion of this plot is a whopping 64%.

Even if you were to try and maximize the space used for the square garden beds the best percentage of arable land that you would get would still only be 36%, almost half that of the keyhole garden.

So, it makes complete sense to build these rather than waste valuable space constructing their square counterparts.

A common recipe for a successful keyhole garden is a ratio of 3:1 in the composition of brown and green material which forms the core garden and breaks down rapidly due to the heat generated by the natural decomposition

Possible Browns

Thin-layer brown materials such as:
Dry, yellow or brown leaves and brown
Grass dead, woody stalks or plants
-
Any paper and wood products: chopped
Twigs, shredded newspaper, phone books, programs, a little slick paper is okay
-
sawdust
-
dryer lint, vacuum cleaner waste
-
Straw
-
wood ash from fireplaces (not a lot)
-
lots of cardboard

Join The Bucket Brigade

- 100% cotton, wool, or silk

Where to find browns:

- Cardboard: furniture stores, appliance stores, hardware stores and some grocery stores.
- Newspaper: ask at local newspaper offices, post office for phone books and junk mail (avoid plastics)

Possible Greens

Thin-layer green materials such as:

- kitchen scraps from vegetables, melon rinds, eggshells, and fruit
- coffee grinds and tea bags
- freshly cut green leaves and grass clippings
- manure
- inexpensive bulk pet food

Where to find greens:

- Coffee grinds with natural filters: coffee shops and restaurants.
-

Join The Bucket Brigade

Fresh manure (barnyard kind): landscape supply yards, horse stalls, or cow barns (avoid vet clinics

DON'T FORGET: Planning ahead for plant selection aids the decision of where your keyhole garden should be built (sun, rain, prevailing winds, house, shelter, etc.)

Yet another example of the concept is incredibly simple, slow, small solutions adding up to provide complexity, stability and abundance.

FOSTER`S DISASTER PLASTER

A weed is a plant that has mastered every survival skill except learning how to grow in rows. ~ Doug Larsen Be a weed.

       Thinking about how things were often referred to back in the day, I remember that folks used to call some medical remedies a plaster. Now depending on its use or the healing intentions of a plaster, this word can mean several different things; it also varies by locale or custom. It can be used as an old fashioned word for a Band-Aid for example or a remedy like what usually comes to most people's mind is the old fashioned mustard plaster they would stick on your chest for bad colds or flu.

       Anyway one way of dealing with a mishap or trying to deal with a disaster is to put a temporary or permanent patch on it. A plaster if you would. Having such a remedy on hand for the conditions one may find themselves in a bug out location without an already prepared garden can be the difference of you making it or not making it so I would strongly advise you to consider adding one of my personally designed seed selection plasters to your B.O.B. gear if survival gardening is part of your disaster preparations or intentions.

I came up with the notion or carefully crafted concept of what I now call my original copyrighted "Disaster Plaster" survival planting method using common wild edibles when I looked over my small heavily wooded 3 acre property and the thirteen 10x4 foot raised beds in my garden and asked myself the question "what would I do gardening wise different from what I am doing now if the shit had just hit the fan?" How would I greatly increase my yields?

My answer like most people I know who are "Bug In" prepared type preppers or part-time homesteaders who are planning on staying wherever they are during and after a grid down mega disaster for a long period of time, will answer "Plant Like Hell!" Till up any bit of extra cleared land I can and sow about all the seed I have on hand except for my reserves!"

Go crazy wondering to myself if all those old seeds I been hanging on to just in case of such an event might sprout or am I just wasting space and time fooling with them? Germination rates on those things would be impossible to guess but I guess they are a measure of hope in some way. Be glad that I had some backup seeds stored in nitrogen even if the varieties were not what I was used to growing.

Go crazy like the Chinese do in a famine and plant corn right up to the telephone poles! Start raking the hell out of leaves in my woods and doing the big compost pile I never got around to. Slash and burn where I can by imitating the time honored but very destructive gardening practices of the indigenous peoples of the rain forests in South America and various geographic areas of Africa. Wait a minute now I am getting carried away. Now what is the first and best thing I can do to insure my success and get a gauge on my seed viability and germination rates?

I will finally get around to building that emergency green house I have had in back of my mind with some tree limbs I got using that roll of clear plastic I have saved just for this occasion in my prep shed. Then I need to round up all the empty spare containers I have like left over nursery six packs and gallon containers, foil roasting pans, egg crates, you name it and fill them with soil and start seedlings! They can start growing long before I get my newly cleared ground ready to plant with seeds and be back up or more controlled growing condition transplants,. That's the ticket! I got my plan coming together now. But something just does not seem right? What might that be?

"Oh hell!" I exclaim to myself. "Dirt, where the hell am I going to get dirt to fill those empty containers? I only have about one 50lb bag of potting soil and part of another left. Now readers please note I grow about 90% organic around here at Prepper Shack but the soil I am on is pitiful and if you are not raised bed gardening it you can't grow anything but a blister at all unless you add some fertilizer of some sort.

The soil is played out terrace farmland that nature took back with forest but its maybe only a ¼ of an inch of topsoil, red dirt, sand and then hard clay. The land actually slides if you disturb it and try to make a bed. I have 2 bags (50lb each) of 10-10-10 on hand as part of my preps and also use it to fertilize my fruit trees, berry and nut bushes. That is the cheapest most efficient way I can attempt the task. I use a small military pick shovel to dig with every early spring before they put leaves out to amend the soil so they stand half a chance to grow and by that I mean it literally. I permacultured the devil out of this place when I first got here and continue to try to add to it. Bug In gardening anyone?

Well money was short and dreams were big so I got dozens of fruit and nut tree seedlings off eBay as sets which averaged about 7-9 inches tall and planted them with a handful of potting mix and the soil from the hole they were being planted in and forgot about them for a few yrs while I tried to keep 10 good 6ft or better trees alive that I had purchased for about 20 bucks a pop. Two and a half years later my bigger orchard trees are producing fruit but not as much as they could. Maybe because those commercial fruit tree food spikes are so expensive and if a tree was supposed to get three or more I only gave them one and now with my economics being stressed again once more I couldn't afford that.

Yes I can be considered a poor man but an adaptable and honest one, and yes I could of done some crazy do it yourself organics to help all my trees along but life and laziness said no that wasn't happening. I also have the philosophy that when it comes to permaculture on my land that I plant something and let nature and it decide if it thrives or dies while I be a bystander and observe and research what does well or doesn't through my "set it and forget it "land conservatory practices I am wont to do to find out what type of flora and fauna grows best on this peculiar soil I have naturally and without much care or intervention on my part.

DISASTER PLASTER

Digging up a bunch of dirt off the property to fill all those containers can be done but it would be a laborious pain in the butt that may or may not grow something. I know that yellow squash will get about 5 inches tall and blossom and die planting directly in it from dry land farming experiments outside the normal soil amended kitchen garden. But now is a good time to admit planting Seminole squash on the edge of the orchard grew without any help by me and if I attended it marginally with some weeding and fertilization my success would have been better.

Anyway I know my land and what is needed to be added where and why on it. One little section of your land is not the same as everywhere else on the same property. I originally planned before contemplating and then writing this book to pretty much go bat crap crazy on day one of a known long term grid down situation evaluating how I could expand my growing area, to maximize my yield by adding more labor intensive but organically sound growing practices on my forlorn dejected and unmanaged guerilla gardening survival planting plots to minimize my insect and disease risks using every primitive and modern trick of gardening I knew in hopes of success.

You see I have been curiously screwing around and doing hands on research for over thirty five years of taking everything from a shovel to a tiller to a patch of uncleared ground and planting things and observing the results be they good or poor. I have learned the majority of soils I have encountered both on properties I have owned and on friends generally will not produce vegetables without some kind of soil amendment.

DISASTER PLASTER

Hence, having a good balanced fertilizer on hand like a bag of slow release 8/8/8 etc is essential if you don't have organic materials like manure to build your soil. I also keep some on hand if something needed side dressing to increase yields or combat problems because of deficiencies in a new bed I am building up. Although I don't like chemical fertilizers and prefer organic gardening methods, in a grid down hit it and get it situation you are a dang fool if you haven't already gone out and spent about $15 for a 50lb bag of good commercial agricultural grade fertilizer while it is cheap and available. You can always trade it or get a neighbors garden started in the worst of dirt, its called survival, right? No time then to get picky about whether something is organic or not when the wolf is howling at your door.

That being said, I started to wonder. Doing all that commercial or homemade fertilizer style gardening is what I originally had set out to explain how to do and what I would do myself to expand my organic garden or have a means of growing if I had to bug out personally.

Except for some elaborating on this theme and adding some homemade organic fertilizers that you could make in the field I figured I would have covered the subject of bug out gardening sufficiently but I felt compelled. That's right I said compelled to stop spending so much time on that subject and instead tell you something that is pretty dang profound and a way to starvation proof yourself.

Did you know that there are 13 edible plants that are found everywhere on the planet? That's right! I can go from Alabama to Alaska to Finland to Jordan to Australia and find one or many more of these species of plants growing. I can find them in the inner cities; I can find them in the suburbs or on a barren road median. The means of mine and your survival is basically nothing more than eating the weeds!

Yea I know, everyone knows that there is an abundance of food in backyards and roadsides but those botanical field guides are confusing and hard to read to let alone memorize right? You want to have this knowledge, you have an identification guide of North American plants maybe you occasionally look at and try to remember and take to the field for some practical hands on learning.

There will be time for all that later you shrug and take some small comfort in having it in your preps and can't wait to attend a meeting with a decent naturalist to point some things out in the woods on a hike at some event you plan on attending. You watch YouTube videos and sometimes force yourself to listen to just about anybody occasionally to pick up some information on whatever plant you decided you were driven into investigating but that whole wild crafting, herb gathering plant identification thing has got you still real hazy about it all and there is just not enough time to learn everything now, right?

Well I would say a lot of us have approached the art of finding some pot greens all wrong. We spend so much time looking for some obscure plant or deciphering scientific texts we don't look right under our feet for a solution.

Do you know who is probably the best naturalist or wild food gatherer you got in your neighborhood? That old man or women up the road who is constantly out doing some gardening and digging up weeds. Most of them don't even know they have the master's eye for identifying edible plants. They will tell you they see weeds, what type of weed it is, its growth habits, how hard it is to eradicate it, what it means your soil is lacking in nutrients that the presence of the weed indicates, what is the best natural or chemical way to kill it, etc. but like I said most don't know that pesky weed can be what's for dinner.

The other guy or gal on your block that you might seek out who knows a bunch about the weeds in your neighborhood or state is one of those chemical lawn guys you can bug for identification with mixed results.

A lot of them get educated in identification of noxious weeds and their control, but on the same note a lot more time is often spent on memorizing what the chemical is that gets rid of pretty much everything and how to sell you a contract so they can spray that crap all over your lawn and house stairs.

Misaligned weeds like the dandelion are waged war upon in every neighborhood but somehow or the other they persist somewhere else.

See you already know one edible plant very well, Dandelions! The whole plant is edible. Oh yuck! You might cry remembering some uninformed common childhood warnings, that white sap in them is poisonous! No its not, you can play the dandelion flute if you want! So now knowing that and maybe looking up some further facts that you can use the roots to make a bitter tasting coffee substitute you begin looking on this lowly weed a bit different. You find it has tangible value as a survival food procurement skill. Something that you are confident will increase your chances of survivability that is easy to spot confidently by you when present.

    I got to thinking about how blessed I was to have my little piece of land that I am hopefully going to be living out my life on and have had the chance to experiment on and try building up my garden soil organically every year and pondered my original hypothecation of "How does one explain how to build a bug out garden?" and concluded one does not focus on that aspect. I fight with the weeds on my property all the time by hand or mechanical means because I wish to increase my vegetable production but you might say I have been blessed because I ain`t sweating having them around.

    The reason being is that if I had crop failure caused by drought, insects, disease etc. at least one of those darn weeds I have been wrestling with would grow in profusion from my neglect and mother nature's nurturing and I would be eating greens and tubers anyway if I was forced by circumstance or just plain wanted to for nutrition or health.

    I know a lot of my weeds in my gardens walkways and I know that which are edible and or medicinal, I also know that many are mostly better for me to be eating than the more tasty and more demanding veggies I normally consume or grow. Nature is a great gardener; she beats me to the punch every spring and already has her wild plants out in spring with tender shoots ready for me to eat before I even put the first shovel to the ground to plant a seed. There is pretty much something out there in the garden to eat long after I say I am done for the summer or decide I don't want to do a winter garden again this year.

This concept got me to thinking and rethinking about what would I do if the poo had hit the fan and I had to abandon my farmstead and bug out with nothing more than an entrenching tool and selection of so called survival seeds.

What skill set do I need to share or hone myself to accomplish this task? I have a decided advantage in surviving through wild plant identification but that is only from mostly studying those 13 plants that occur everywhere that a whole lot of folks don't have a clue about. I could research and list attributes for those buying farmland about what the weeds on it said about soil quality but that could be an injustice.

I had 25 acres one time that had at one time been a hog farm. The guy had planted acres of purslane on it and after disking it in and tilling and planting cover crops etc it still plagued me and my garden. Purslane is called pigweed because lots of people planted this stuff for the hogs to root up and eat.

In a "I want to just be farming regular herbs and vegetable world" purslane is a scourge and noxious weed, in a SHTF world it is my most prolific and nutritious reliable food source, my medicine, my untended bounty. It's rare to find an entire field full of it but I have never seen a field without it and in profusion. They herbicide the hell out of the side of a lot of roads but it persistently still springs up. I would rather not eat it from such areas but no telling how long after it was wiped out it was brought back in again from the wind or birds and animals to grow anew.

If I had to just pick a bug out location wouldn't it be cool if I started with an abandoned farm field that had lots of weeds growing in it? Better yet, some of the tastier weeds growing in proliferation? Yea, that is what I am going to do when I am out and about, start spying for and paying attention to places with an abundance of edible weeds. Hell, if I was able I would sink my bug out garden right down in the center of a good weed patch after I had gathered the edibles for that day's dinner and tomorrow's fertilizer and bug in and start gardening!

I know fighting with the weeds will be a daily chore for awhile but at least I can eat what I am weeding and waiting for a more civilized vegetable to grow. That's another thing about these thirteen weeds, they follow along growing where ever man has settled and dwelt. We kind of have a symbiotic relationship with them you might say. That is if we can understand and recognize them for what they are, then we have a survival garden often times already provided by mother nature, but man likes to play with his environment and regional tastes. Likes and dislikes eradicate this survival garden in order to provide for lawns or big agricultural fields that change the landscape.

I continued to challenge myself with the question of what should I do day one of a disaster and examined what it was that I wanted most from my desperate disaster gardening plans and came up with simply more edible weeds!

DISASTER PLASTER

They require no extra fertilizer, are drought and pest resistant and seem to be pretty much a carefree survival solution. All I have to do is encourage the species I prefer and continue to discourage those I don't.

Instead of tilling up and breaking a lot of sweat working more land while burning more calories I can't afford with the impending food shortage gearing up, while expending my precious little bit of extra gas in my preps I have stored and diminishing other irreplaceable resources trying to force the land to grow my more recognizable vegetables, why don't I try expending minimal effort working with mother nature instead of working so hard against her? I already know she has the upper hand and usually wins in the end.

If I want more forageable dandelions to be growing on that strip of unused land in front of my street that only occasionally gets mowed due to my freedom of living on a dead end country road, then I figure if the lights go out for months or years why not throw a bunch of dandelions seeds out on it instead of trying to think what might grow out there with the few seeds I got left from planting everywhere else?

For that matter if I was forced to bug out somewhere and start anew well then I know I would wish I had me a bunch of dandelion and other weed seeds to jump start any empty plot of land I had access to. That is when it dawned on me to make such a seed grenade. Eureka! Oh a commercially packaged conglomeration of wildflower seeds exists as well as those that grow grass from those grow it anywhere lawn patches but no one to my knowledge has ever come up with a proprietary blend of edible weed seeds to tip natures scales in their favor and thus my invention of the "Disaster Plaster" was born! I had come up with a simple and cost effective means to insure my survival and others that had been eluding me even after my many years studying emergency management and practicing my prepping and homesteading.

Not just any weed seeds would do and not just any seed company would be the one I chose to private label or co-pack for me. Being astute in the private label business as well as being networked into the commercial seeds men servicing the prepper community and backyard gardeners, I made contact and through much deliberation and resourcing came up with an offering for "Disaster Plasters" that I am proud to present to you for your purchasing consideration. You could assemble your own or maybe even do some wild crafting and get some seeds for free but if you want a ready made solution with high germination rates and the proper species mix, please try mine. You can find my seed selections at Kingsmountainseeds.webs.com.

King's Mountain Seeds
The Orginal Disaster Plaster
"Just Throw And Grow!"

A word of caution is in order regarding what a lot of people and some governments and agencies consider to be noxious weeds. Handle with them care and in some states you will find certain laws apply so please make yourself aware of any local restrictions that might apply to your area. In other words don't get stupid and try growing your entire backyard in edible weeds etc. unless it is truly a dire emergency that needs a plaster on that disaster. Your neighbors will thank you and so will I.

Personally I don't want one single seed of the blends I have managed to put together to touch my soil or fall upon my carpet for that matter. I often joke that I feel like I need to put on a hazmat suit and enter a clean chamber every time I mess with making up a packet of throw and grow. I treat them with due respect because to not treat them so is to invite a possible disaster.

I am a country boy homesteading, dirt digging farmsteading prepper playing hobbyist with all kinds of rare vegetables and herbs while attempting to grow the biggest organic tomato in the county for bragging rights and less weeds means less work and more satisfaction as well as success.

A bunch of extra weeds could spell failure to some of my less tended vegetable and rare plant plots or permaculture endeavors if I get a bunch of newly introduced voracious growing weeds to contend with. I got enough weeds of my own without purposely or accidentally introducing a new host of others, but after close study of a disastrous grid down, humanity ending, societal collapsing, dire survival situation that I recognize as a possible threat or risk, I opt to have on hand my nemesis all prepackaged and ready to go. Famine may visit but starvation won't be able to take purchase at my door as long as I have access to edible weeds.

While you can pretty much guarantee most likely that everyone from prepper to farmer to sheeple is busy freaking out on just what they are going to do next come apocalyptic grid down, I have my own iron clad preparedness plan and it is I am happy to say as fool proof as Mother Nature herself in my opinion. Nothing is fool proof in this or any other world as we are all unfortunately well aware of but when it gets down to trusting dumb luck and seeds that don't seem to mind finding their own way to a sidewalk crack in a big city and growing and thriving regardless of conditions then I say that my plan is looking pretty good about now.

For those of you not adept at plant identification, it will be a saving grace to you to have on hand this book in printed format (or write down the fertilizer recipes if you just have electronic versions available) and a "Disaster Plaster" because hands on education in identification comes with that insurance policy in the form of wild edible food. You will soon be able to identify and recognize many forms of edible weeds in their various stages of life by seeing and doing. These skills will serve you well and expand your newly found survival skill expanded foraging territories that include pretty much most anywhere you might be walking around at someday.

By reducing my traditional gardening methods through using this back to the land human assisted innovation, I now have lots of time to get my indoor preps in further order. Oh, I still have a few chores I need to do increasing my truck garden type vegetable production here and there but mostly it will be business as usual except grabbing a couple of tea bags full of weed seeds and doing the sprinkle the seed shuffle here and there on some of those places I have identified as having potential for an edible weed crop and go back inside to wait this calamity out.

DISASTER PLASTER

The property will fast go looking unattended and overgrown, faster than the few weekly mowed plots around me anyway that will now probably sound like every tiller in America just cranked up all at once soon as the survival seed packages finally get used if folks got them with mixed results.

Oh the music of my tillers engine will also join the fray as that plot of soil I was going to eventually turn into a garden gets a lick and a promise with the addition of some commercial fertilizer and maybe some topsoil but I will be done with that and planting in a day.

Sprinkling my little Disaster Plasters on the soil with trepidation and a smile works wonders for my soul because I know that if I got everything wrong about today and planting a new garden I will still have accomplished an amazing feat.

I said with confidence, Mother Nature please feed me and provide for my needs and for others and I am 100% sure she shall. Weeds excel at being in survival mode, that's what they do best and they do it best by not having anyone but the wind and the rain helping them along.

No fertilizer and no tilling. Well, we might count some of those sidewalk crack growing weeds taking advantage of a rich limestone environment from the concrete but no one planted them there or try to mimic it as a gardening method although someday in a chaotic future I can imagine Mother Nature having a field day breaking up concrete with ever persistent growth of plants that will no longer be trod upon daily by humans as nature retakes her domains.

DISASTER PLASTER

If I was forced to bug out I would certainly heed my own advice on a bug out vegetable garden but I wouldn't be waiting for it to produce to feed me in 60-90 days. No I would improve upon my situation first by upping the ante that I would be able to find shortly for myself an augmentation to the roots and herbs I was dependant on for daily survival until a crop came in by selectively salting the ground with food producing perennials that did not require my further attention after throwing them to the wind upon their appointed places.

My now newly weed enhanced and overgrown land areas that would give horrors to herbicide companies and my pocket book to try and control is now well managed by me using nothing more than my desire to eat and graze upon its abundance. I eat it, I tear it out by roots to consume it or make tea and it decides that loose soil is a perfect place to establish new growth or introduces a new weed I would be less likely to consume but has other amazing attributes I can study.

My formula for the ideal disaster plaster to put on my land can vary by local soil types, seasons and weather but rather than just customize for my own needs its easier and more beneficial to choose what mix of seeds works best for me universally in any climate and weather. Stick my choices of seeds into a blend that is a no-nonsense solution to my woes of bug out gardening and I have everything I need to garden successfully in an apocalypse.

I need to eat day one of any kind of disaster and my recognition of the weeds that try to take over my garden every year at home teaches me how to survive anywhere with or without doing any agricultural endeavors myself. This principle, this hard won knowledge that I feel compelled to share with you is not something new or brilliant, no indeed hunter gathers and country folks have shared this knowledge for centuries one way or another. But modern folks like you and I haven't been exposed to such wisdom and it's as obscure to us as operating a computer would be to a mountain man. There is nothing about it that seems innate or self-explanatory because we don't observe the same signs they did to look to for their survival.

They observed nature, climates seasons and weather and observed what plants and animals were doing all their lives often times. They asked indigenous peoples less advanced in technology or known commercial agricultural practices what was working for them and discovered many new economically viable species as well as heightened survival skills.

It wasn't that long ago that the majority of people here in the U.S. lived on a piece of land where we got at least part of our subsistence out of but yet with all the hunting and agriculture skills evident in the generations of the great depression millions disappeared off the roles of the census of that period by presumably starvation and or malnutrition related diseases.

The knowledge base of home gardening or identifying wild edible plants is no longer a common attribute and if the same economic calamity happened today the results would be horrendous. Food stamps didn't exist back then and programs like Social Security, minimum wage, Medicare, Medicaid, prenatal nutrition etc. didn't exist either.

DISASTER PLASTER

Now that we are living in a society where -----out of 10 get food stamps and ---- out of ten are dependant on some form of government assistance we get about 1/3 of the folks living in the U.S. or a hundred million people who can't make it on their own now this minute.

Take into account a kind figure of 10% of the population having some mental issues requiring medication, the border line nut jobs we all know not seeking treatment, that the U.S. has more people in some seriously messed up prisons than any country in the world learning how to be nastier than when they went in, add your diabetics, cancer patients or other chronically ill folks and the factor that 60 % of everyone doesn't have more than a weeks worth of food stored and available if they are cut off from the grocery store or the bank and you get at least 200 million zombies that statistically speaking don't know you can eat a dandelion but would be willing to give grass a try if they were starving to death. How many would turn cannibalistic and be willing to give you a try for dinner remains to be seen.

The unknowns and ramifications of a supply chain global famine without outside aid are not well studied but have predictable results. It's bloody chaos that takes about a century to get over if history is an indication before civilization as we know it starts back up again and enough people are still around to write poems and songs that the artists try to reproduce in their renderings of how truly bad things are when we forget how to survive the past calamities and how lowly weeds or animals saw us through these hard times.

Fate is fickle and unrepentant about sorting those folks out that fail to adapt to change but is much harder on those that fail to remember past lessons in survival. The old axiom that "Those who fail to remember history are doomed to repeat it" always rings true and those who have no knowledge of the old time wisdom involved in surviving in distant lands or climes will fare no better.

We can learn a lot about survival off grid now if we stop to monitor our own newsworthy headlines but most people do not take the time to register or research such facts in evidence. Look at Syria for example at the date of this writing which has 80% of its people living without power for more than 900 days. How about the lessons of Bosnia, Herzegovina torn apart by civil and religious wars, add in the strife and war in the Congo every few years and the constant droughts occurring in Ethiopia and Somalia and begin to see a pattern. People live on what they can and what they know before civilization or aid arrives eventually to gather up the remaining survivors looking for some food security under often times slave like dependence to a new regime.

As long as you can eat something you still have a choice of acceptance or rejection to policies no matter how bland or bitter tasting your alternative might be but as a collective let me explain a history lesson or two old Ben Franklin warned us about and we should always remain vigilant about and remember. He stated that and I am paraphrasing "Those that give up a little bit of liberty for a little bit of safety deserve neither" and these words echo in my head as the government bureaucracy allows GMO foods, enhanced pesticides, non reproducible vegetable seeds and other Franken horrors to occur while also trying to control the very liquid of life and outlawing the collection of rain water while allowing an oil fracking crew to pump enough chemical laden water into your environment to cause earthquakes and your tap water in the community to catch on fire in one of those "oops" mistakes that happen and get buried in the media without a whimper from the majority of the unaffected at the moment community.

The Russians were, and still are, a master of controlling those that don't follow the states Pogroms and mandates and intentionally starved millions to death in what used to be the breadbasket of Europe for farming wheat and other grain crops while the peasants tried to find enough weeds if they remembered them to survive.

Always remember that food is used as a manipulation and proof of power by government agencies that seek to suppress dissent. Freedom and thoughts of revolution generally speaking come about when the controlled government subsistence to the big corporation or state run cooperatives to live up to the promise of plenty for the dependant population after years of regrets and strife from moving from an independent or consumer driven economy.

Bread lines, charitable soup lines, etc. follow economic as well as agricultural collapses on a national scale, on a personal scale they can occur as quickly as tomorrow with job loss, homelessness and a variety of other incursions.

Can you find food in the city or the country for yourself with no outside assistance long term? No, most of us unfortunately can't nor most of us would be healthy or resourceful enough already to undertake such a challenge yet we see people attempting it every day whether from need or premonition of something big is going to happen to our food reserves and economy.

The writing is on the wall, charitable food banks are understaffed and have increased demands that are not being met, homeless shelters are already filled to capacity when available, cities try to hide their homeless by busing them else where or creating laws that it is illegal for a private citizen to give them aid or sustenance. It is a tragic and mean spirited world we live in that is only getting worse as the haves and have nots try to distance themselves from each other and human kindness in general.

What if everyone that was homeless knew 13 plants that were edible could be found and eaten and that they didn't have to beg for food or break a law to survive? Would that be a place to start to end a few injustices in this world? Self assurance and reliance in the worst of times that means you can retain your own dignity and resiliency no matter what happens because you have a choice and the knowledge to compound that into something different if you so desired?

Governments and dictators fear this, it removes you from the "system" and it is hard to hold you accountable for anything more than just living by your God given rights to gather food and subsist. You are no longer a tax payer a government education indoctrinated factory worker that punches the man's clock everyday to increase the coffers of the elite and the fascist or statism values they promote to insure their powers over you.

Sanctions, the headlines are alive with sanctions on one country or another of the worst humanity offenders while those that impose them bicker about tariffs and other economic advantages amongst themselves that reflect upon the quality of life its citizens endure. If you could be assured you and your family could eat tomorrow if you didn't get a paycheck this week would you be more apt to layout and sue for regress over unsafe working conditions or wages?

Of course you would if you deemed it truly necessary for a change to occur without already try to work out your grievances in a chain of command manner without a work stoppage. Unions got their foothold this way before politicians and crime bosses took over the collective purses the workers created to support strikers and screwed the concept up but the controlling factor of being able to get food to live another day remains. What if we were all working say at a lumber mill and had farms to go home to and being self sufficient food wise wasn't in the cards for the owner to wait the strikers out.

How about the concept that you know you can be dropped off on a street corner or side of the road anywhere and be able to sustain yourself to some degree food wise no matter what? Would this change the way you look at life or prep for the future? Try it for a day or two if you're able, try it just mentally for a moment now without actually having to do it.

Can you find 5 edible plants in 5 minutes that could possibly sustain you today? Would you dare to even conceive of such a thing?

A lot of people think that winter and summer squash has something to do with the best time of planting but that is not true, they can be planted at anytime. The term refers to storage ability or fresh eating. Some squashes keep longer like Butternut etc. and some are better for fresh eating like yellow squash, zucchini etc. because of their short shelf life.

    You should be growing both types. You should also be thinking about where you want to store your excess crop of shelf stable squash and pumpkins because you're going to need to rely on its bounty later. This is where the idea of bug out gardening begins to teach you some staunch lessons in reality.

    Now I am going to introduce to you a type of squash called "Seminole Squash" which can last a very long time as a basic staple. (I had one on a kitchen counter for a year and a half and it didn't start rotting until the stem on the end broke off. A paper towel patch on the stem scar added a few months to its continued freshness." Seminole squash is a very old heirloom said to be raised on little island hummocks in the everglades by the Seminole Indians.

    They look like little pumpkins growing on very long vines, often the vines get to the length of 30 ft or more. Anyway as they escape your backyard and attempt to go down your driveway you realize they take over a lot of real-estate for a much smaller yield than you would expect.

    What to do with whatever is not used or given away is not really a problem because it's only a few extra small pumpkins per vine but they take up space. Thinking about putting in extra vines and ending up say with a months worth if you were forced to eat one every day because that would be all there was soon has you revaluating your planting area and wondering where you're going to put 30 about 9 inch pumpkins. Another squash I like to grow is jumbo pink banana squash; these are a large heirloom variety weighing up to 30 lbs or more. Now add 20 or so of these long squash to your stash and you see we are starting to have a little problem that is if you can grow that much surplus in a season and have added some other food options to get you through winter and the time before next planting and harvest.

The best place to store lots of different kinds of root crops is underground, either leaving them in ground until needed or storing them in a manmade structure like a root cellar. My favorite pretty much self storing and self seeding survival food crop is Jerusalem artichokes which ironically have nothing to do with Jerusalem or artichokes, lots of folks prefer to call them sunchokes by the way. These prolific good tasting tubers are an almost ideal prepper food.

A pound of sunchokes for planting can be purchased for around $12.00 and could arguably be the best and cheapest prep/food insurance you will ever buy.

The seasons you could possibly be facing of you bugging out or remaining bugged in pretty much cannot be chosen or closely anticipated. Yes the credo of preppers is often quoted as preparing for the worst but hoping for the best means you will be most likely stuck at home or in the field in the middle of winter with no chance of planting anything but that doesn't mean there is nothing to do in the garden until spring. There are many tasks you can undertake for preplanting

DISASTER PLASTER

5

Bug It In! Bug It In!

"A society grows great when old men plant trees whose shade they know they shall never sit in." --Greek proverb

Give these simple recipes a go if you find any unwanted insects crawling' around your precious plants.

Homemade All-Purpose Insecticide Spray

The Ingredients

- 15 cloves garlic
- 1 onion
- 3 cayenne peppers (or 3 jalapeno peppers or 1 tablespoon cayenne powder)

- 1/2 teaspoon liquid castile soap (fragrance free)
- 4 cups warm water

Method

1. In a blender combine the water, garlic, onion, and peppers and puree.
2. Pour the mixture into a glass jar, secure the lid, and steep for 6-24 hours on the counter.
3. Strain through a cheesecloth, then add the liquid castile soap and mix well.
4. Load the mixture into a spray bottle and you're good to go.

To Use

I love this recipe! Try it on a host of pests in your garden and feel free to adjust it as needed with other insect repellent herbs. Spray the tops and bottoms of the leaves, thoroughly coating them. Store this mixture in the fridge and if it is strained well, it should keep for at least 1-2 months. *Note: Be sure to test a patch prior to spraying the entire plant. Take care not to get this on your skin or in your eyes, the cayenne pepper will burn.*

Basic Insecticidal Soap

The Ingredients

- 1 1/2 teaspoon any type of liquid soap (i.e. castile, dish washing soap, ivory, etc.)
- 1 quart water

Method

1. Combine all ingredients in a spray bottle.

To Use

Set the spray bottle nozzle to stream and spray infested areas of the foliage. This insecticidal soap works great against some of the most common garden pests such as: aphids, earworms, borers, mites, whiteflies, maggots, moths, and beetles. *Note: By adding 1/4 cup of isopropyl alcohol to the above recipe you can create a very mild but effective insecticidal soap that treats scale insects. The alcohol works against the scale's shell.*

Spider Mite Spray

The Ingredients

- 1/8 cup buttermilk
- 1 cup whole wheat flour
- 1 1/4 gallon of water

Method

1. In a bucket combine all of the ingredients and mix completely.
2. Load into a spray bottle.

To Use

Spray this homemade Spider Mite Spray anywhere spider mites are living or crawling. The mixture should rid your garden of all types of mites.

Notes

Before you set foot out into the garden to eradicate it...get to know the insects in your area. There are so many bugs living in our little backyard ecosystems — otherwise known as the garden — that are beneficial and need to be protected. Knowing which bugs are there to help your cause and those that are there to destroy it is a very important part to harvesting a successful crop.

Alcohol spray for <u>Aphids</u>

Mix ½ to 1 cup alcohol with a quart of water. Do not spray the entire plant until you have done a test leaf. Spray one leaf. Wait a day. If it shows signs of burning, do not use alcohol on the plant. Never use in the heat of the day in the sun.

Beer Traps for Slugs

Put some cheap beer in saucers. Place the saucers every 3 to 4 feet around the plants that are being eaten. The slugs will crawl into the beer and drown.

Chamomile Tea for Damping Off

Spray seedlings with a hot water infusion of chamomile tea to prevent the disease.

Citrus Spray for Aphids

This is a good spray for aphids or any other soft-bodied bugs. Boil 2 cups of water in a glass or stainless steel pot. Remove from the burner and add the peel of one lemon or one grapefruit. Cover the pot and let steep overnight. Mix ½ water and ½ citrus liquid. The spray must come in contact with the insects' body to be effective. Spray as needed.

Eucalyptus Liquid Soap (found in health food stores)

Add ½ teaspoon to a quart of water and spray for insects.

Horticultural oil

These sprays have a petroleum distillate carrier for natural botanical insecticides. Never use them on a sunny day, and be sure plants are watered well before spraying.

Insecticidal soap

Sold under the Safer brand name. You will find it in any garden store. The concentrate is a better buy than any others.

If you are using only molasses, stir into water and use. If using all ingredients, mix molasses and powders and make into a paste. Wrap 1 cup of the paste in a panty hose. Put in the water, and let sit for 2 to 4 hours. Strain and spray.

Three Sprays for Powdery Mildew

1. Mix ¼ teaspoon baking soda with a quart of water and spray every 2 days until it is gone.

BUG IT IN! BUG IT IN!

2. Mix 1 ½ TBS baking soda, 1 TBS insecticidal soap, and 1 TBS canola oil with 1 cup water. Add 1 TBS. vinegar LAST, otherwise it might bubble over. Pour into a sprayer that holds more than a gallon. Add a gallon of water. Shake or stir. Spray plant covering tops and bottoms of leaves.

Mix 1 gallon warm water with 3 TBS. baking soda and 1 TBS. Murphy's Oil Soap. Spray plants as soon as you see a grayish coat on the leaves. Spray every 7 to 10 days until daytime temperatures go up to 70 degrees. On plants with chronic powdery mildew problems (bee balm, phlox) use this spray as a preventive. Spray once or twice in early spring before it appears. If you notice it, remove all affected leaves, spray with this solution, prune or trim to improve air circulation, and make sure the plants are not stressed by other problems like drought. Stressed plants are susceptible to diseases and pests.

In order to live off a garden, you practically have to live in it. ~Frank McKinney Hubbard

SURVIVAL SEED SELECTION

"The seed holds a very great secret—it never gets old. It is the eternal YES to life."
—Anat Vaughan-Lee

The trend to eat organic fresh foods for health reasons started in part due to the media and whistle blowers public ally speaking out on the hazards of the Franken foods and GMO seeds that somehow became part of the mainstay of American as well as many other countries daily diets.

The facts are out there and this author won't politicize or belabor the well known facts about the hazards of such a diet as the reader is probably well versed in these facts or can easily look them up on the internet or observe the news. A critical fact that remains, that is not normally discussed, is that the foods we eat today lack in key nutritional elements and food values of

SEED SELECTION

only a few years ago. The evidence is in and it's well documented that a tomato for example you buy in a grocery store contains far less nutrition than a tomato grown in the 1970s. It doesn't matter if you are looking at field grown, hot house, hydroponics or ripened on the vine the results are all the same, organically grown or chemically grown heirloom tomatoes generally have anywhere from 1/3 to one half more of the nutritional value of the commercially grown hybrids.

We won't get into the factual intricacies that various hybrids or heirlooms have their own specific set of nutritional characteristics at this point of the book but suffice it to say that one tomato is not a standardized FDA daily nutritional requirement that you can lump all tomatoes under. The same goes for all other vegetables and this factor is often overlooked when choosing or selecting seeds for the home garden.

The title of this book was going to be called the "Survival Garden Tower" book for a reason and introduce you to the concepts of vermicomposting and worm towers as a means of creating a sustainable organic garden. The primary focus and title evolved into many systems on how to grow a garden quickly and sustainably, yet the seed selection is not a one size fits all approach in choosing the content and variety of seed you will plant as you plan for a disaster or a victory garden.

One thing that comes out of the volumes of research done to study the effects on the human body of eating various GMO foods is what specific parts of the body are affected by shall we say their odd DNA or selective chemistry. I am generalizing here and stating a layman's opinion so if the scientific facts of this statement

SEED SELECTION

need clarification feel free to do your own research and form your own opinions. The reason I bring that up we know from medical research that certain flavonoids, etc. that are contained or not contained in a vegetable affects certain parts of the body fits with the survival theme of this book.

You might say "Ron that doesn't matter I just want to grow a "quick and easy" heirloom garden and will get enough nutrition from that" is true but it is not the best preparation or healthful thing you want to do.

I would say that 99% of you reading this book are Preppers anyway so I don't need to tell you or elaborate on different expected disasters mean prepping with different things. Yes, generally speaking, if you prep for one thing it covers most everything else in one form or another but we all have certain expectations and needs we associate with specific disasters.

Take for example a gas mask, I don't have one prepped although I have a world of military experience with using one simply because in my objective opinion that I don't have a particular concern of an event happening that is on my list of likely events to occur that I will need. Yes, if I had myself a bunch of extra bucks or saw one cheap at a yard sale I might end up with one for a "what if" scenario but I can't really rationalize it or miss it when I evaluate my personal state of preparedness.

When I look at those medical reports of what GMO or Non GMO, etc. plants do for or to my body I start thinking first on what is in here to help advise me of my own personal needs in any disaster that might affect my wellbeing.

SEED SELECTION

Let's take for example when the diets of the survivors of the nuclear disaster at Chernobyl or the horrific after effects on survivors of the bombing of Hiroshima and Nagasaki occurred.

I, like other scientifically minded people, wonder why some people were more or less susceptible to certain diseases are afflicted and if you discount closeness to the blast or fallout etc we eventually get down to diet. Are there any major differences in vitamin or nutrition uptake that I can put my finger on and definitively say that the addition or removal of any one common food, vitamin or chemical component increases or decreases my chances of surviving radiation poisoning?

I have a nuclear power plant 180 miles from my house and prepping for it melting down and reducing any complications I might get if it did might be a concern if say I was worried about that fact or a dirty bomb going off in a major city like Atlanta which is a few hours away from me also occurring.

I could also go all out doomsday prepper (I don't like that word much) and build me a bunker for that matter but again, time, money, expectations or probability of likely events classifies my purchases accordingly.

Let's take a minute and say that you have all those concerns and do the ultimate preps for them. You bought you a Geiger counter, you were fool enough to spend too much money on Potassium Iodide (Not necessary or effective over a certain age, see footnotes) or you own the whole shooting match of NBC field gear to survive in that environment as well as have enough food not to have to

SEED SELECTION

plant or worry about the fallout particles in rain for years and think you are pretty well set.

I, on the other hand after much deliberated study, found out that green leafy vegetables naturally remove some of the toxins caused by radiation as well as helps the body recover from such an event and applied my energy and wisdom towards finding out what plant and which variety accomplishes that task best and prepped accordingly.

"Essential to survival, seeds have profound spiritual implications. For centuries the planting of seed in the earth not only nourished humanity, but also symbolized the mystery of life and the journey of the soul. In our current supermarket lifestyle of pre-packaged products, far removed from the cycles of planting, we have nearly forgotten this mystery. Now as the integrity of the seed is threatened, so is its primal meaning." These words are taken from the new book, Sacred Seed: A Collection of Essays

It was found in Russia as well as numerous peer reviewed articles in Japan as well as the United States that Kale, already being considered a super food, had almost miraculous results over other prescribed and accepted radiation treatments.

So I buy kale seeds for my preps because it makes sense that my choice of "survival seeds" includes a variety known to have higher specific nutritional attributes for its variety than others to improve the physical health in humans exposed to radiation. Perhaps certain varieties

SEED SELECTION

exhibit traits like drought or insect resistance for my geographic area that others don't? I weigh these characteristics and my reasons for growing them and formulate my own seed storage system based upon my own needs or disaster expectations.

If for example I planned to keep a pack of kale seeds in my bug out bag because I was worried about my health or others in a radiological concern situation, I would want one that was hardy in most climates and undemanding in cultivation, on the other hand if I was dependent on a truck farm for economic considerations or wish to establish a permaculture situation then my choice of varieties could vary widely. It takes many years of trial and experimentation in any given local area to choose what is best for you but the idea is to be able to recognize your preparedness needs and act accordingly.

"That sounds simple enough on the surface and you can certainly follow my catch all varieties known to thrive in most areas to plan your own seed reserve but you must also take into account taste, form, planting conditions and many other factors specific to your needs.

For example, my mom is on that horrible but necessary pharmaceutical Warfarin (same chemical in rat poison) and can only eat kale in regulated and prescribed ways. A little internet research tells me the main components of one variety over another has less chance of adverse reaction so since we enjoy eating kale from my kitchen garden I grow a variety less susceptible to interact with the manufactured drugs that sustain her heart.

SEED SELECTION

This is my response to my own personal environment and disasters but yet I balance and temper my responses accordingly. I do not grow a variety if its culture is too demanding or not suited to the purpose it was planted for but instead plant several and observe its propagation and resilience to seasons and pests.

A prime example of this theoretical application of analyzing space and resources is the addition of permaculture to your normal garden plot. This hit or miss way of trying to accomplish your own "food forest" is one that will go against many peoples psyche of nurturing and tending their kitchen gardens but it is one that deserves tremendous consideration because you will learn more about gardening as a "dry land" methodology dependent on nature and weather conditions versus a human interaction model that requires regular watering and weeding.

The only way you will know know what works well and will grow like a weed on your property is from experimentation, observation and reasonable assumptions by saying the hell with modern farming or gardening methods and just putting in a plant or some seeds down in an area that you will not be babying and mothering along.

Kind of a plant and forget situation as you first come upon a piece of land that is likely without too much effort to produce something on its own without human hands and time to be successful. I call it "If it grows it grows and if it don't it don't" which drives everyone who offers help or advice to my latest gardening efforts in a 'scratch the dirt let's see what happens' way of learning my land a bit crazy. What most people fail to grasp is that

SEED SELECTION

I don't just do this haphazardly and without a great deal of thought mostly.

My 40 plus years of seeing what naturally grows in an area or what likes to threaten or pester my garden as a weed already tells me a lot about the alkalinity of the soil or growing conditions based upon what I see that certain kinds of so called unwanted weeds are flourishing under and under what kinds of conditions they thrive or die off under.

I can't write this information down for you except for some generic guidelines I will give you for common soil generic conditions that are prevalent in most locales. Instead, I greatly encourage you to go experiment for yourself and learn the laws of nature and the lay of the land on your own behest.

Do this research for yourself well before an emergency happens, but if you say I can't or won't do this action: then you need to have some quantitative or qualitative basis of evaluating your seeds laid out for you as comparison other by me. This is the same knowledge you could get on your own possibly but I trust you to critically think about my questions as expertly and academically being developed in order to serve a purpose just the same as you do say explaining you're beloved EDC (every day carry) pocket knife.

You will never be able to pick a variety that will grow the same way and under the same conditions every year no matter how much you agonize over it or research it. This is true even if you take all my years of experience and have the agricultural extension agent in your pocket

SEED SELECTION

for any area that you may find your lucky self bugged in or out to will it ever be the answer to what you need the moment the balloon goes up or the grid goes down.

The reasoning for this is because of the simple fact of nature that nothing is consistent. The weather is never consistent, your soil gets depleted, if you don't rotate crops you can get disease, a 100 year plague of locusts might visit, etc. and it is only with diversity, good planting practices and patience will you be able to depend on your disaster garden to augment your preps.

Take for example that I live in the hot humid Deep South and every year like every garden or commercial farmer down here grows yellow squash and prepares to do battle with all the nemesis inherent in my state to wipe out this mainstay of farmers markets and southern cuisine. Squash borers, blossom end rot, powdery mildew, etc. is all poised in the nature of things and expected to ruin my harvest and us gardeners experienced with such calamities who declare war with these things every spring are hoping they don't happen but are getting ready for the inevitable losing the war against them but are planting anyway because "this year" we are going to try this or that in hopes our plants don't quit producing mid-season.

"Oh, the crops produce for a bit and you get sick of eating the abundance and then like a light switch going on or off approximately the same time of year here comes the crop failure or plant exhaustion setting in and you can see the signs everywhere if you actually visit those fellow gardeners fields that are still producing of an encroaching malevolence of known or unknown origins threatening.

SEED SELECTION

The seeds for a "Bug Out Gardener:" have as many considerations to deliberate as the type of gear you want to stick in your bug out bag or pack in your car. The problem with seeds though is that they are not universal say like a sleeping bag to accomplish a certain task but there are similarities. For example when choosing a sleeping bag you must account for temperature ratings for your geographic area and indeed cold hardiness of plants must be considered but size is also important. That is where the most scrutiny must come in when choosing a plant variety, bigger is not always better in many ways.

Preppers planning on creating a bug out garden from scratch would be well served if they also possessed in their seed reserves varieties of vegetables that were specific for container or patio gardening as well as a hard look at specific "bush" varieties for field crops. Therein lays the crux of the confusion of what to get because a large majority of the dwarf or bush varieties are hybrids that may or may not be suitable for inclusion in your seed wallet.

Now we have already learned that just because something is a hybrid it does not immediately exclude it from being included in your preparedness gear. If it is an open pollinated variety it will reproduce true and saving seeds are not a problem so don't discount these scientifically enhanced but non GMO predictable producers.

The selective process of choosing or cross breeding varieties that are naturally resistant to diseases, weather conditions, size, productivity, etc. is just well regulated smart approaches to insuring that you will have a viable as well as economically beneficial crop under a wide range of

SEED SELECTION

conditions. Always remember first and foremost that hybrids are developed with the farmer or commercial grower in mind to produce in the best or worst conditions.

It's about the money, who can be first to market with produce, who can have an extended harvest, reducing the needs for pesticides or fungicides, etc. so choose accordingly amongst these marvel plants as long as they're open pollinated and you will increase your survival chances.

That is not to say these types of varieties don't have their draw backs the same as heirloom varieties. Take for example tomatoes, as a general rule most determinate tomatoes (those that grow to a shorter specific height) produce all the majority of their crop over a short period of time and the lifecycle begins to end whereas indeterminate varieties (those that grow large and wildly) will keep producing over a much longer season and will give you an extended harvest.

There is a place in the garden for all varieties but unlike the homesteaders' garden where space and time is not as critical, the so called "Bug Out" gardener does not have the luxury of trying out what works best for his or her plot of land and will find themselves greatly lacking in resources and time to afford themselves much of a margin for error in their seed selection judgments. You are stuck with what you have variety wise and the seed you plant this year will most likely be the only choice you will have to save for many years to come, so choose wisely and diversely.

Land is a funny thing and what works 10 miles up the road from me isn't guaranteed to produce the same

SEED SELECTION

results as what might be grown on mine. The first thing I want to look at is adaptability of my variety to a broad range of conditions. If we are in a "hopefully never" bug out situation and we are forced to grow some modest crop of vegetables to try to sustain ourselves, it is very difficult to say what soil and weather conditions we will be facing once we arrive unless we have already surveyed our bug out location and those results and mother nature will likely throw a few monkey wrenches into the mix to put a royal damn damn on our expectations and realistic results.

If you have never planted a seed in the ground you plan on bugging out to, you might as well say your stuff is not going to grow without some divine intervention or some great operator insights. That is what this book is about, not to leave you with wishing or praying for your plants to grow or make you a master gardener (I am certainly not), no it's all about avoiding common gardener or operator errors and allow you to choose wisely or with a modicum of knowledge about 'how stuff works' so you can be more confident and resilient in your efforts.

Prepping for a survival garden to be set up in an unknown location requires you to be able to put on your thinking cap under your boonie hat before you set off on that little suicide mission of bugging out you're going on and think failure is an option and how am I going to overcome that. This requires a lot of thinking outside the box and a great deal of personal introspection on what types of conditions you yourself and your family personally expect to face and start saying over and over again "Plan A, B, C", etc. without most folks penchant for not honestly facing some very hard realities.

SEED SELECTION

"Let's get the notion of just digging up the soil anywhere and planting a seed and getting something, anything to produce even if it is only one tomato or ear of corn out of the way. It don't work, it never works and I have been trying it for over 40 years, every year in one form or another as an experiment to observe the results in everything from girlfriends backyards, farm hedge rows, abandoned farmsteads, out in the woods, my front lawn, etc. I also have tried it with buying bunches of expensive commercial soil thinking it was a reasonable assumption I would get better results.

Let me tell you a few quick gardening stories here and admitably everyone's results will vary but listening will give you a lot of insight and might just save you a lot of anxiety and expense.

About 10 years ago I had moved back to the city and had talked a good friend into letting me contribute to making their backyard into a raised bed garden wonderland of growing and sustainable things. Now I had just got this lady to convert to being a fulltime prepper and this idea seemed to be the normal progression of the preparedness attitude even with her dire warnings that this particular backyard previously had been tilled up once or twice years back with abysmal results. "Oh no, not to worry I say! We will do it in raised beds and bring our soil in to insure results. I had many years of successful experience with literally an acre of such beds so success was guaranteed, I optimized. It didn't matter that we soon found out if you dug a half foot into the ground you would find bricks everywhere in that yard that evidently had been land filled or an old house had been torn down upon or both, we were growing on top of this crap and it shouldn't matter. First things first, place had a bit much

SEED SELECTION

shade so an attack on the vine grown edges and overshadowing tree limbs was undertaken to let Mr. Sunshine in better. Then a conversation was held about what to build the proposed boxes out of, money was tight but a pair of those damn usury high interest rate credit cards from a big box lumber and home supply place was available so we thought at that time the wise frugal but functional decision would be to use thin treated but cheaper decking planks to construct our folly.

Now modern technology like screw guns was available but not having such and being old school I duplicated what I knew to be best and grabbed my worn out old leather nail apron, filled it with them twisty galvanized ardox nails, holstered my big wooden long handled framing hammer and set to work busting my ass in what I considered was the laziest knowledgeable and experienced way while entertaining the neighbors to building a beautiful landscaped arena of about 20 boxes.

Mostly they were 10x4 using scaled lumber which for a couple bucks I got the store to saw 8 footers in half for me to save time to attach to standard 10ft lumber but I also had 6 5x5 beds in the mix done the same way. When I was constructing these I thought how smart I was and how much less time and effort it took to construct these raised bed boxes versus what I had left back at my old farm I sold. Those things are probably going to outlast me as they were made from 2 to three inch thick oak 14' to 16' x 8" unmilled rough cut boards I had found sitting as pallets 6 ft tall basically forgotten and blued with age in back of a lumber yard. Those damn things were like a piece of furniture that petrifies with time and had turned almost petrified to rock and required drilling a pilot hole to just get a nail into them. It didn't matter if you soaped the

SEED SELECTION

nail, put them in with a sledge hammer, bought cut nails etc. you had to break down and use a drill and it was easy to burn a drill bit up if you weren't careful.

Anyway the new 5/8 decking plank boxes were built and I figured we would get at least 5-7 years out of them before new solutions had to be implemented so no worries (2012 was on the horizon in a couple years and I was prepping whether it happened or not) but unfortunately when I sold my place my tiller went with it and so the slow "I been working on the railroad" routine started with me swinging a mattock and preparing the beds by hand. (If you haven't read my book "Possum Prepping" and the need and wisdom for always having such a tool, go get it, particularly if you don't have one already and consider yourself "prepped".

Well, luckily I was a younger man but an old one anyway that was used to swinging one of those damn things and experienced at making the tool work for me instead of the tool working me and got the ground busted up and a bit raised for all 20 of them rock pile boxes over two days. While nursing new blisters and fending off requests for neighbors thinking about getting me to help the neighbors put in a garden or remove some shrubs, when I got done with this project we started plotting and scheming how we were going to get all those bags of dirt we needed from the big box store home as well as paid for.

I had me a 1985 Blazer at that time which had taken more trips with lumber strapped to the roof or hanging out the tail gate hatch than I cared to sustain the gas cost again for so we kind of chipped away at it

SEED SELECTION

piecemeal as the voracious dirt eating boxes could understand.

Authors note, I don't care what the measurements or the line of sight reasoning says, add 5 more bags of dirt to whatever calculation you came up with per box and find yourself wanting and further in debt. It settles. It disappears; it's got low places, etc.

Now about this time everybody had a sale on so called garden soil and potting mixes and the private label companies that had just got into the business and the Wall street marketers must of seen everyone coming and got advice from the seed catalog folks to influence us to buy because beautiful bags with labels such as "Jungle Mix" etc. offered pictures and prints of lush growing gardens that forever changed the hobby gardeners results and landscapes for the worse. Little did we know that hurricane Katrina was the reasoning to this madness that remains in the store offerings today? You see there was hundreds and hundreds of miles of destruction to feed the coffers of the sacked dirt business with ground up tree or probably house debris.

They grind up the trees in wood chippers etc. and get paid to haul it to FEMA stations where some old guy stands on a platform that can look down into an eighteen wheeler trailer or regular clean up truck or trailer to prevent fraud and call it a load so you get paid for hauling it.

What's under all those branches he don't know, if they been floating in that cesspool of industrial chemicals, oil and Lord knows what else for weeks or months, he don't know and he don't care, its not his job, it all goes

SEED SELECTION

into the fill. Then some industrialist, agronomist, etc. comes along after its been sitting awhile on land FEMA either leased or bought for the cleanup and says hey buddy, let me take that off your hands and gimme a grant to make it environmentally "safe" by composting it and plants to produce so-called gardening soil sprang up everywhere.

What happened was, and read any label you want to in the big box stores, was that the "Top soil' you were buying unless you read the label's small print, doesn't contain any "soil" unless you count sand which is also added for weight and might be ocean sand containing salt for all anyone knows was piled on in profusion in every garden everywhere to fulfill the dreams of unaware gardeners everywhere to try to increase their harvests.

Woe and shame be upon those that contrived such a fraud upon society and shame to their heirs profiting from it but this practice continues. You might think hey composted wood certainly should be able to grow a garden and it can if it's part of an ecologically sensible balance of soil amendments, that is why I busted up the soil to mix in with it before I started dumping dirt in my boxes so that I could get whatever good nutrients already in my soil to add to my applications but plain composted wood sucks, take my word for it.

You see, the majority of what you are buying out here if I get you to read labels is "soil less" soil. Sucks don't it? Its basically better suited for weed control versus growing vegetables unless you are adding chemical fertilizers and lots of water or finding out what variety of weed is prevalent on your property that likes growing in that crap. Finding real dirt, real compost or real manure is

SEED SELECTION

becoming impossible as the people that used to supply it age or get out of the business as peoples misconceptions about advertised commercial products increases. Remember what is sold as organically grown in the U.S. has tons of loopholes and meanings.

So now back in that backyard we are talking about, I got probably about 500 bucks worth at least of questionable pretty whacked so-called dirt that's not dirt and won't hold water very long, lacks nutrients and biodiversity and my boxes are not even well filled.

As the years go on it gets worse as various solutions are tried to improve it by adding blood meal, cotton meal, bone meal, etc. in tiny gardening store bags if you can find it to the 18-27% credit card bills coming in for buying that other crap that now needs some vermiculite or something just to hold water for more than a day or two and those dreams of gardening and that overabundance of left over seeds I bought from the gardening catalogs that paint my dreams every year in spring time kind of start disappearing.

If you already did the same bad purchases or planning, you already know we can eventually fix it and us home gardeners are a hearty breed known for our patience and persistence but you can't experience this learning curve in a grid down situation. If you want to fix what you already got now or foresee starting up from scratch elsewhere by all means go to the vermiculture part of this book and begin preparing now. It's cheaper, better and more dependable long term than anything else I can recommend. Notice I didn't say short term but there are benefits there also.

SEED SELECTION

This section of the book is dedicated to seed selection and although my diatribe earlier might seem to be off the mark, it is very important for you to realize that soil conditions and diversity are the only way you can overcome poor growing conditions.

This type of knowledge is only obtained by knowledge and experience through observation of many seasons and diverse growing conditions. When you are starting your first garden anywhere or for that matter trying to improve upon your own soil and harvest, eventually you will come to the conclusion "I am only going to do what works for me." If you had no success your first year you tend to look at the obvious for answers, oh we had a drought this year, the bugs were really bad, I didn't know that lack of calcium caused blossom end rot, etc. but something grew and it grew well so you say to yourself I am going to plant more of this and less of that next year etc. and the cycle begins again. Congratulations! You are getting this trial and error gardening mentality and facts of production down pat. That is why farmers specialize, that is why many heirlooms still exist but things are not that cut and dried.

For example, I grew nothing but Better Boy tomatoes for my little truck farm for 25 years with great results. Everyone in my community pretty much did the same and I was one of those gabby farmers you could sometimes bump into when you're looking at plant varieties at the nursery or big box stores that would share the advice of main crop farming. Now as far as I know and 6 more seasons of buying frigging plants occasionally to get the instant garden fix and including a huge range of grumbling neighbors and farmers that that variety no

SEED SELECTION

longer works in spite of decades of knowledge gone kaput and expected more surprises on the horizon.

I say vehemently that the fix is in my griping, educated but lowly held opinion and that whatever strain the nurseries are selling now, at least for my area anyway have been transformed in some way from what I had successfully planted for many seasons before.

This attack of the non producing tomatoes coincided with the big added growing soil fiasco so maybe something in that crap is detrimental to that variety and not others but that makes no sense to me.

I even give the conspiracy section of my brain a nudging and poking at me about the so called killer genes many hybrids or GMO laced varieties contain so they don't reproduce if you try planting the seed a second year. Either way, I had to change from tried and true to saying what the heck? This ain't my first rodeo, I know exactly what I am doing and my normal methods of getting the biggest and best maters in the county no longer worked and changed varieties to the others I had planted before with success or that other growers used as their mainstay.

The Better Boy Tomato in my conversations with other planters and my own personal trials and tribulations after much success previously growing this variety in all types of conditions was doing something odd. The variety now grows abundantly in foliage but does not produce any or very much fruit or if I sprinkle my monkey dust of gardeners tricks on it to shock it into production appears not to be near as prolific as in the past. I put this down initially for a number of reasons but primarily because of

SEED SELECTION

the big bee die off we were experiencing and eventually broke down and bought some of that expensive hormonal blossom set to be able to at least produce something but I had other varieties of tomato that were unaffected without the use of the hormonal heavily labeled warnings spray.

That plants pretty much now in my area only come from one big nursery and they typically sell nice quality goods I got to place the blame on genetics now. One truck farmer friend of mine still grows this variety and with great success but he has been saving and replanting the same seeds for many years and has not introduced any new plantings. That's the old way to insure your success, save the seeds from the biggest and best and make your own hybrid if you want to call it that that thrives under your farms conditions and is adapted to your soil.

Now when the Better Boy tomato fiasco was going on and my growing capabilities were being questioned I had six hybrid Bush Goliath tomatoes growing I wanted to try out and they will produce consistently and productively pretty much everywhere myself or my friends have tried to grow them and for appearances sake I like them around with their huge stems, short height and consistent production but they are a hybrid and have two traits I don't like.

One thing I don't like in particular is they sometimes have an almost hollow like tendency at times for a seed cavity and although they stay ripe on the vine pretty good they have a short shelf life and will soften and rot quickly once picked. Yes I can produce tomatoes dependably and in abundance but I am not proud of them and although by no means do I do the tomato taste

SEED SELECTION

aficionado thing, my joy is to hear Ron is a good consistent truck farmer of sorts when he wants to be.

    I like that folks are saying my tomatoes are the best tasting they ever had whether they are lying to me or not for giving them fresh farm raised organic veggies. Took me awhile to get them to just say every tomato I gave those benefactors of my largesse to quit saying every tomato I gave them no matter what variety tastes wonderful and tell me exactly which one they liked best and why.

    I always try to grow an abundant surplus and whatever is not given away or sold tastes the same to me when squished and flavored up for canning some spaghetti sauce. Now fried green tomatoes are a whole another matter to me and I get my chefs hat on when it comes to what I prefer and desire with salivating appreciation for the first green tomater of spring the garden observers allow me to have versus ripening into a red slicing mater sandwich that they have been waiting for.

    I am an aficionado on that particular art of southern cooking lore and green maters and fresh eating maters as well as if you batter or don't batter in your recipe is a matter of cooks pride in every household in my area. I have half a dozen or more ways to fry a tomato based on variety, taste, how much flour, oil or corn meal we got in the house on a given day, but to go to fried green tomato heaven and make them up for a competition it has to be slightly acidic. This variety lacks the acidity I want to give you that "bite" I like in my cooking, not the sweetness some desire in a fresh sliced sandwich which is

SEED SELECTION

not high on my list and falls under apocalyptic food like eating wild mustard greens.

Now all these factors except for the hybrid versus non hybrid etc., might not matter to some and I have been hearing, I guess just for the last 3 years now, that folks just want a homegrown tomato because they have done everything from reading books to buying commercial fertilizers and have marvelously green plants that produce nothing would I please just tell them what to buy now and how to do it.

I can hang out at the bar in the BBQ House and say let me take a look at what you are doing or float you a couple suggestions for a beer to bring in a bumper crop, hybrids, heirlooms and the weather and the bugs willing but in a truly grid down situation you all are dead and tomato bereft. I will ask you first what variety you are growing, say oh hell for a certain few, not argue with you that the university tested heirlooms you are trying which are not heirlooms to me because in my opinion they are relatively new and never worked for me but for the price of another beer or if I have mercy on your soul say here, try these seeds and shut up and grow something new to you but old to me and run back to my farmstead for some seeds.

That means you ain`t got no tomatoes of any sort and it don't matter what variety you planted if it doesn't consistently give you produce to sell and profit from or food for your table.

By watching diverse varieties of supposedly the same vegetable and how it acts and reacts to conditions or for that matter carefully reading about the attributes of a

SEED SELECTION

specific strain you realize that your judgments predicate your success in an endeavor the same as purchasing good hiking boots but not thinking to break them in before a long hike will bite you in the butt no matter what the cost or that the waterproof hype they were sold to you with was probably written by the same guy that told you about that tent you found out leaked badly on that one and only camping trip you went on.

What is the point of all this you are asking? Don't just plan on growing one thing and don't believe everything that is written or told to you. Either hands on experience will save the day or get knowledgeable so you can assess your failures and make adjustments with some country prepper wisdom because you are aware of some of the pitfalls of putting all your eggs in one basket.

I might suggest to you a variety that may in poor conditions only give you say 7 tomatoes all season but that beats no tomatoes all season and if you can keep yourself from eating the biggest fruit and save the seeds from what was grown on your land over those climatic and soil conditions then you have a better chance of a bigger and better harvest next year that will be more adapted to your soil and weather conditions than the original seed that you planted.

Farmers have been doing this for years, save the best for seed and eat the runts if that's all you've got. Eventually, you will find that you have the most perfectly adapted and productive variety for your soil and growing conditions by carefully choosing the biggest and the best producing plants grown on your soil to regenerate again the following season from your careful observation and selection.

SEED SELECTION

After you got this part down pat, you no longer have to closely observe and the mainstay of your tomato crop will continue to reproduce true without any other intervention by the grower. You have done it! You might have even bred a new variety but you are now extremely confident in your resources and your land to make a nickel next year and eat well.

Reading seed catalogs will give you a great deal of insight about what's out there or the resistance to diseases you never heard of but it will also add to the confusion of choices and give you a disease that is as bad as any would be prepper wanting stuff and spending too much money already. Damn hobbies are costly, prepping is the worst and reading seed catalogs in the dead of winter with the promise of spring is even worse as we marvel over all those pictures and drawings of succulent fruits and vegetables and forget last years' disappointments.

We guess, we judge, we speculate about how a certain variety will grow in our own garden and then the panic attack sets in and you buy one of those "survival seed" packets just to have backup after carefully comparing and analyzing every variety in it. Before you waste your money, well it's not a waste actually, anytime we have ourselves a bit of something that always beats a lot of nothing.

Think about it for yourself now that you have gained a bit more survival garden knowledge, would anything in one of those commercially assembled packets be your first choice of a variety that you would want for your bug out garden and why? Why is it none of your first choices appear in the package contents and is there any

SEED SELECTION

particular attribute to the seeds offered for sale that reach out and grab you or teach you something that you have not considered?

The answer at this books writing from all the offerings I have seen is, no they won't. You will get a paragraph on heirlooms versus hybrids which is something that you already probably know but will read anyway, Non GMO will be emblazoned everywhere they could put it but if their heirlooms or open pollinated you knew that anyway, a small list of just the seeds follows or a couple lines of text about the variety will be made available if there is enough web sales space available and now your left on your own to either research more or trust the "survival seed experts" hand selecting and selling you that variety.

That can take lots of hours to look up everything, that is if you actually take the time to research that list just to find out what each variety is, ponder if it is right for your area, how much filler it contains (a lot of corn often times BOO! Unless you know how to grow it) in that thousands of survival seeds thing in some kind of thrifty nifty packaging you could probably buy cheaper and fill yourself with what you actually wanted for varieties. So unless you got the money to just shelf seeds that you will never get around to growing or end up with wildly mixed results if you do, just stop and think first before you make that purchase!

You can consider buying my seed offerings and I hope that you do, or you can go buy some of the seed variety's I suggest from someone else and second guess germination rates or if they were produced in China etc. Or you can look at this whole survival seed variety

SEED SELECTION

choosing quandary with eyes wide open and carefully choose what you think will work best for you.

I don't wish to create undue mistrust or apprehension about the industry in general but suffice to say I talked to a number of current seed buyers and suppliers for the industry and got a pretty accurate idea about how it all works. The companies don't grow all their own seeds and are dependent on smaller trusted growers to supply by contract the requirements of their label.

A lot of these smaller growers have done this task for generations and a lot are new or are headed up by a new generation of growers and results are not always consistent. There are also many tiers in the bulk seed business where one major supplier or producer will sell down the line for a growing season and drought or other growing conditions will affect supply. New introductions of hybrids affect demand as does growing practices of the large commercial farms switching to a variety that say will stay green longer so the food plant operators and grocery store suppliers can zap it with ultraviolet light for hygienic or ripening reasons before passing it on to the end user consumer.

Weather is a factor none of us can control but as preppers most of us can relate to our own states general weather patterns even as crazy as the climatic changes we have been experiencing are likely to occur.

Of course I got bit in the butt one year when it snowed in Alabama and ruined most of my tomato crop one year when I didn't have the money or time to replant. On the same note I didn't run out the following year buying Canadian seeds meant for a short growing seasons

SEED SELECTION

that a week or two of my possibly predictable 100 degree weather and no rain would have had probably had extremely adverse effects on them when another variety I normally grow could have shrugged it off.

Yes, I tried a few of the cold weather offerings because I do the diversity grower thing and was curious if they might have some dual attributes and my results weren't catastrophic until midsummer but it was a short lived variety anyway so you might say the results were inconsequential.

Of course a variety that likes hot humid weather and a long growth period of many hours of sunlight probably would have been killed by the first frost in Canada so my standard varieties would do nothing for survival in that territory.

The seeds I am suggesting in this book as well as those you might find on your own when choosing a survival seed bank should be able to adapt, be proven to adapt in several climate zones, provide a normal reasonable yield and not focus on a bumper crops or size without pesticides, fungicides or lots of chemical fertilizers or water requirements and therein lies the dilemma. Just like there is no miracle bullets for your guns there are no miracle plants that can do it all but there are many that can serve the purpose and excel if you do your homework.

Like guns and ammo you need to protect them from excessive moisture but there are simple things you can do to protect them. Generally speaking, those old time paper seed packets stored in normal household conditions will last 4 yrs. If you want to spend more on packaging for them to be guaranteed by the manufacturer 5 or more

SEED SELECTION

years go ahead and spend the money or take that dollar and put the paper or glassine envelopes in a big Mylar bag you probably already got preparing for EMP or other catastrophe and you can increase your chances on surviving by using good judgment and practical knowledge applications.

If four years of seed viability and decreasing germination probability doesn't suit your prepping plans adjust accordingly but wouldn't it be better to have a well chosen seed over a generic so called prepackaged survival seed? One chosen for your own growing conditions but that is adaptable to travel and grow states away from your general locale?

A lot of seeds can last longer than that 4 years mark suggested because they have harder shells or temperature requirements etc. Always smile to yourself and be optimistic about such remembering that scientists took a few grains of wheat out of an old vessel in an Egyptian tomb and they sprouted and grew!

Of course as preppers we don't expect such miraculous events and plan accordingly but on the other hand we don't throw out old seeds as being worthless. If some divine or natural intervention will ever happen regarding old out of date seeds it will only occur if you first took the effort to start with something and plant them!

TOTALLY TOMATOES AND A TOUCH OF SQUASH

A PREPPERS PERSPECTIVE

Did you know?

Tomatoes are thought to originate in Peru. The name comes from the Aztec "xitomatl," which means "plump thing with a navel".

The star or centerpiece that is talked about in most gardens is the quest to raise the ultimate tomato. There are scores and scores of different varieties of both hybrid and heirlooms to choose from and new varieties are introduced every year as seed saver gardeners, Seed bank offerings, commercial planters and nurseries all compete in this immortal quest.

Tomatoes varieties are chosen to be planted by consumers and producers to be grown for all sorts of purposes. The seed and young plant offerings come in a

Totally Tomatoes A Preppers Perspective

dizzying array of varieties based on various sizes, shapes and colors. Tomatoes that are bred for or naturally have special attributes that lend themselves to be better for home canning, making sauces and pastes, adding to salads, slicing for sandwiches ,hot weather, cold weather, fresh market ,shipping, the list goes on and on.

Tomatoes made to be grown in containers, Determinate (only grow to a certain height range) Indeterminate (grow to any height range) potato leafed, non potato leafed, Sun, drought, and crack resistant etc.

Tomatoes with or without a built in resistance or gene to off set a variety of common diseases and viruses as well as a host of other maladies. Before I get into what I consider the best choice for a bug out garden or any other kind for that matter let us cover a few ways you can enhance your yields in a bug out garden.

Because tomatoes are naturally acidic, vinegar can be used as a natural fungicide as well as a fertilizer on these tasty and nutritious plants. Vinegar is a natural substance that has a wide variety of uses. It is acidic, but not toxic, which means it is safe to consume. For that reason, it can be used on edible as well as non-edible plants without harming them, as long as it is used in moderation and diluted with water. Vinegar also has many other uses that you can refer to in my recipe, hints and tips section at the end of this book.

Tomatoes are known to be prone to fungal diseases, especially during periods of wet spring weather. A combination of apple cider vinegar and water can

Totally Tomatoes A Preppers Perspective

prevent and treat leaf spots fungi, mildews and scab diseases. Combine 3 tbsp. of cider vinegar with 1 gallon of water. Put the solution into a spray bottle and spray your tomato plants every morning if you have or encounter this problem.

You can fertilize your tomatoes with a mixture of water, ammonia and vinegar. Combine 1 cup ammonia with 2 cups of white distilled vinegar, then add it to 5 gallons of water. Use a watering can to sprinkle this mixture over your tomato plants and the surrounding soil. Do this about once every two weeks in the spring. This will encourage fruiting.

One problem many people have is that their plants produce blossoms but no fruits. This mystery can be caused by a variety of things but I blame the mysterious honey bee die off that we are having in this country as well as many others for several years now. As of this books publication fully 50% of the bee population in the United States have died off.

Remember What Einstein Said Regarding Bees

"If the bee disappeared off the face of the Earth, man would only have four years left to live."

Let me tell you about a tomato I consider a great bug out or prepper tomato. It produces red fruit on strong

Totally Tomatoes A Preppers Perspective

plants that have proven to take all sorts of abuse with little ill effect. Great for beginners and negligent gardeners. Fruits contain up to 2 1/2 times the usual Vitamin C.

PERON... THE WORLDS ONLY SPRAYLESS TOMATO! Can be grown in any condition and still performs very well.

These tomatoes are sort of rare these days so check my web site for current offerings. I would hazard to say that after my reintroduction and recommendation in this book that they may become more scarce as very few seed catalogs list them as a regular offering.
KingsMountainSeeds.webs.com

Widely adaptable strain – from the tropics to Alaska. Peron has gained a reputation as one of the easiest to grow red slicing and processing tomatoes over the past 40 years. Peron was also rated better than Brandywine for taste.

Introduced 1951 by Gleckler's from Argentina. Called "Sprayless" because the vigorous vines needed no treatment. Tasty red tomatoes on disease-resistant vines. Produces a high percentage of uniform, defect free fruits, 3-4" in diameter. Flavor is sweet with some intricacy. Reliable, flavorful, and a garden mainstay.

An early tomato 68 days. (Mostly known as Peron Sprayless) It's less interesting other name is just plain "Sprayless".
Compact, semi-determinate in growth vines are fairly disease resistant. Deep-red, dual-purpose canning

and slicing sort. Smooth, slightly oblate fruits are very dense-fleshed and meaty, and show very little core. Skins are very thick and tough, simplifying peeling when processing, and making the crack-resistant fresh fruits keep extremely well. Flavor is very good and sweet enough for fresh use as well. Developed prior to 1954 by Prof. Abelardo Piovano of Argentina. This remarkable tomato was developed by Professor Abelardo Piovano of the National University of Argentina.

Peron is thought to be the most naturally insect resistant tomato of all and thrives in areas where all tomatoes need to be sprayed against insects, without any chemical intervention. The 6-8 ounce red fruit have a solid, meaty interior and the skin comes off easily without emersion in boiling water. Flavor is mildly acid and Peron is a good keeper. Introduced in the US in 1951 by the Gleckler Seed Co of Ohio.

They are moderately large slicing tomatoes which are bright red and are very meaty with somewhat firm texture allowing them to store well for days on the kitchen counter.

Plants are vigorous and highly adaptable to every climate and condition, hot or cold, dry or wet. They are called sprayless because of the plants incredible resistance to disease and fungus allowing it to produce heavy crops of blemish free tomatoes in areas no other varieties can thrive without chemicals.

1958 Gleckers Seed Catalog says about Peron

Totally Tomatoes A Preppers Perspective

Sprayless....

" A miraculous variety developed by Prof. Abelardo Piovano at the National University of Argentina. Medium size semi-determinate bushy vines are very resistant to fungus diseases common to tomatoes. Foliage is semi-dense. A very heavy yielder of large size, slightly flattened globular fruits of the most extraordinary quality. Interior of fruits very solid and meaty, without any core. Very small and numerous seed cells, form a perfect fruit structure. Ripens to a beautiful deep red color over the entire fruit without green or yellow shoulders. Its tough, velvety-smooth skin is very crack resistant and easily peeled without immersing in hot water, a rarity not found in other varieties. Flavor is mildly acid and of a most delicious taste. Fruits keep exceptionally long after ripening. The Peron tomato is called sprayless because it will produce a normal crop of quality fruit in most areas without any disease control. No other tomato was ever introduced that received so many voluntary complimentary reports and we have them by the hundreds. No other tomato ever introduced has shown such wide adaptability. These reports have come from practically every state, in areas where they were unable to grow any other strains. It performs wonderfully in the tropics where the fungus diseases get out of hand. From Alaska we have a report it is wonderful in the greenhouse. Its drought resistance is terrific."

As a prepper/grower I can tell you that this variety is the only one in the world that is said to not require spraying. And no pesticide must be good for you and the

Totally Tomatoes A Preppers Perspective

environment, let alone making it a wise choice for that bug out garden you are planning. It produces excellent quality fruits on strong plants which outperform most hybrids with the fruit containing up to 2 and a half times the vitamin C. A must for every tomato lover or bug out gardener.

Here is a great storage tomato that is even more difficult to find but I occasionally get them from a grower who harvest seeds from tomatoes raised from seed and grown in their garden in Edmonton, Canada.

Reverend Morrow's Long Keeper is a slow-ripening heirloom winter storage tomato. Round, medium-size, light-colored fruits picked in September and October can be eaten in December and possibly even January. Best stored in a cool room. Determinate plants. Provide strong support for heavy clusters of fruit. Days to maturity, yields, fruit sizes and flavors will vary with growing conditions, weather (heat), and length of season. I save seeds from this one.

This one is easier to find but still a rare variety, I have limited experience with it and this text was taken from a seed catalog.

Long Keeper TOMATO, WINTER STORAGE
78 days. (Semi-determinate) Due to the slow ripening characteristic of this variety, fruits become ripe 1-1/2 to 3 months after harvest, ensuring a supply of fresh tomatoes into the winter. Some customers report storing Long Keeper 4 to 6 months. Though the quality doesn't

Totally Tomatoes A Preppers Perspective

match that of a fresh garden tomato, flavor and texture is superior to most winter supermarket tomatoes. Unblemished tomatoes are harvested before frost and allowed to ripen at room temperature.

Store at room temperature so fruits are not touching and check for ripeness and rotting weekly. Used apple boxes with their fruit separators are convenient for this. Fruits are mature for harvest when they have a pale, pink blush. The 4 to 7 oz. fruits ripen in storage to a satiny, red-orange color. Flesh ripens to medium-red. Best planted in late spring or early summer for fall harvest, start seeds in early May.

Long Keeper is often grown as a supplement to the main crop

When should you start tomato seeds?
In growing season Zone 3 which is fairly short. Folks start their seeds indoors in early April and set plants out in the garden in early June, when the soil is warm and the small plants will root in quickly and get off to a strong start. We aim to grow large plants that will remain vigorous and productive until autumn's hard frosts. If you have a longer growing season mine in Alabama (zone 7), you can start seeds at different times. You can sow indoors right through late winter and spring and set new seedlings into the garden from late spring to high summer. Just be sure the soil in your garden is warm when you transplant your seedlings into it, whether this is April or July or somewhere in between.

Totally Tomatoes A Preppers Perspective

Official planting day in the Deep South is Good Friday before Easter although I try to get out earlier with mixed results from a late frost.

And when moving small plants outdoors, do so gradually -- a shady hour or two the first day, three or four semi-sunny hours the second day, and so on -- until they are "hardened off" and can stand up to a full day of strong sunlight. Once transplanted, the seedlings should have a good ten weeks of warm/hot weather ahead in which to grow to maturity.

This tomato was a new introduction to my garden this year and results have been good. I chose it for its attributes which is what I am trying to get you to do with your seed selections. I list here with its seed sellers quotes which I found to be true.

Wild Florida Everglades Tomato

The Wild Florida Everglades tomato is a rare perennial tomato that has the growth characteristics of grass and or weeds. Known for its sweet flavor and its small size (roughly compared to a size of a dime or a nickel). This variety of tomato is very rare, The sweetest! with Little or no acid content and This tomato breed is an Heirloom variety which is NON-GMO all organic Garden high GRADE (My own Gradescale of AAA+++ as a Produce man of 16 years as one of the best not sold in the Market)and has been known to grow on the beach and in the sand! Most of the time with neglect and will adapt to any climates and best of all is this tomato is not available in your local grocery stores. Perhaps in a local Farmer's Market if you are lucky

Totally Tomatoes A Preppers Perspective

Very prolific, indeterminate, and grows in clusters of 6 to 8 clusters in a vine.

This particular tomato is a novelty/specialty and is said to be the original "wild" tomato bred overtime where all of the domesticated bred tomatoes originated from.

I know I called this chapter" totally tomatoes but since we are talking about the impending doom or risks of the lack of bees for pollination will cause it is appropriate have a word with you about hand pollinating squash. I have had to do this on two seasonal occasions and I tell you it worried the devil out of me to come to a new awaking:

I had originally thought that my squash crop failure was due to lack of nutrients in the soil because I had never experienced it before in all my years of producing squash on small country farms.

I had coaxed, cajoled and dedicated resources to my then newly converted prepper girlfriend to takeover her backyard and landscape it into a 20 plus raised bed garden of ambitious and ascetic proportions. Oh what fools we were with Lowes credit cards and cash in hand to attempt this in the old city suburb chosen but 2012 with its ominous prophecies believed or not was two years away and I had sold my old farmstead years ago and had moved back to the city to help out the elderly parents.

Expensive sacks and sacks of store bought dirt went into those beds because I couldn't find a local seller willing to deliver the more natural top soil and manure I was used too to amend the soil. We soon found out that this soil or

Totally Tomatoes A Preppers Perspective

soiless soil made from Katrina recycled ground up trees and whatever else crap would not hold water and calcium and nitrogen deficiencies became apparent. Stupidly but with high hopes and high credit card interest invested in that big name supposedly cure all miracle pre bagged soil that fertilizes and retains water but there was no way to afford to spread it around as much as the manufacturer suggested so we upped the water bill instead until I could fix it next season with more primitive but less expensive methods.

On and on went this disheartening garden fight with the plants and girlfriend losing confidence in me as a old experienced dirt farmer as I constantly searched my memory, asked old timers and store clerks for old or new clues how I could make this obstinate garden produce the yields I was used to have in my many seasons of success. It was getting to be down right humiliating to be reminded that I had already purchased my vendors license and a new set of produce weighing scales with plans to park my old work truck on a likely busy corner and be able to sell off excess produce if I had the desire or need for some extra economic income.

Quite some clues here that made me think I had not acknowledged the obvious for a food source that most squash produces more male flowers than female and that everyone else but me ate them every year as a seasonal delicacy. Hand pollination was the key and eating the extra male flowers.

I wondered what portents or implications this indicated for the state of food security and economics in the world.

Totally Tomatoes A Preppers Perspective

The term **summer** and **winter** for squash are only based on current usage, not on actuality. Summer types are on the market all winter; and winter types are on the markets in the late summer and fall, as well as winter. Thus, the terms Summer and Winter are deceptive and confusing. This terminology was never meant to confuse - it just dates back to a time when the seasons were more crucial to man's survival than they are now. Good keepers became known as winter vegetables if they would keep until December.

Winter squash comes in shapes round and elongated, scalloped and pear-shaped with flesh that ranges from golden-yellow to brilliant orange. Most winter squashes are vine-type plants whose fruits are harvested when fully mature. They take longer to mature than summer squash (3 months or more) and are best harvested once the cool weather of fall sets in. They can be stored for months in a cool basement-hence the name Winter squash.

Totally Tomatoes A Preppers Perspective

My tree Italian tomato setup I built. Eventually I will put fencing on top and teach the tomatoes to hang down to be harvested.

PREPPERS HERBAL

"Let food be thy medicine and let medicine be thy food." - Hippocrates, the Father of Medicine (460-377 B.C.)

Disclaimer: Statements contained herein have not been evaluated by the Food and Drug Administration. These products are not intended to diagnose, treat and cure or prevent disease.

This intended as a reference volume only, not as a medical manual. The information given here is designed to help you make informed decisions about your health. It is not intended as a substitute for any treatment that may have been prescribed by your doctor. If you suspect that you have a medical problem, we urge you to seek competent medical help.

You Can Grow Your Own Healthcare

The history of humanity is rich with the complex interplay between man and the natural world. There are tens of thousands of medicinal plants on this planet, and any condition may be treated by working with them with care and respect.

Adaptogens in plants have great importance in helping us to cope with the stresses of modern day life and support the body's natural defenses against emotional and environmental stressors

There are over 20,000 species of edible plants in the world yet fewer than 20 species now provide 90% of our food. However, there are hundreds of less well known edible plants from all around the world which are both delicious and nutritious.

Heal All certainly has a most self-assured name. You may agree or disagree, but heal-all certainly deserves some attention. The benefits of All-Heal and Prunella vulgaris are legendary, and modern nutritional and medicinal studies indicate that the legends may be scientifically supported. I consider it to be the best all-around medicinal plant and grow it also for nutrition.

Edible, it is chewy and flavorless, more to be eaten for nutrition than as a gastronomic delight. As a woodland grower, it affords good resource for greens to people who hike far from cities.

Properties: Heal-All is edible and medicinal, can be used in salads, soups, stews, or boiled as a pot herb. Medicinally, the whole plant is poulticed onto wounds to promote healing. A mouthwash made from an infusion of the whole plant can be used to treat sore throats, thrush and gum infections. Internally, a tea can be used to treat diarrhea and internal bleeding Used as an alternative medicine for centuries on just about every continent in the world, and for just about every ailment known to man,

This is one of the best-known of all "weeds," not only because it's so common in disturbed, temperate habitats worldwide, including along sidewalks in cities, but also because of its memorable flowers, which are worth taking a close look at, as is done below:

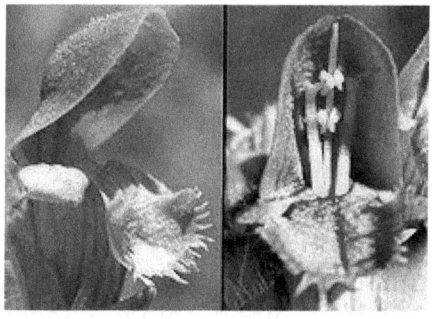

Traditionally, Heal All tea was prescribed for illnesses such as colds and flu, even before cultures

understood what a viral infection was. Today, research by the "Asia Journal of Traditional Medicines" has shown that Prunella vulgaris actually does combat viral infections.

Heal-All, Prunella vulgaris

Other Names: Prunella, All-Heal, Hook-Heal, Self Heal, Slough-Heal, Brunella, Heart of the Earth, Blue Curls, Carpenter-weed, Common Selfheal, Consolida Minor, Lance Selfheal, Sicklewort, Woundwort, Xia Ku Ca

Widely regarded as European wound herb, widely used to stop bleeding. In western herbalism, leaves and young shoots applied to fresh wounds to stop bleeding and as first aid for clean cuts.

According to legend and also Peterson's Guide to Medicinal Plants heal's all will take care of problems with lungs, liver, kidneys, blood, joints, cancers, ulcers, tumors, swellings, and back trouble. The usual method of ingestion is as a leaf tea or alcohol extraction. I also like chopping the leaves up and adding them to any rice I am cooking.

The plant can be air-dried for later use as tea, but the alcohol extraction is best done with fresh leaves. The dried leaves & flowers can also be smoked as part of an herbal "tobacco" mixture.

Is gentle astringency also helps to control chronic and sudden diarrhea (although it is recommended that this application be used under the aegis of a health care provider)

Heal All does not appear to have been known to the ancient Romans or Greeks, but it was mentioned in Chinese medical literature during the Han Dynasty (206 B.C.- A. D. 23) as an important herb in the treatment of complaints associated with a disturbed liver, high blood pressure and conjunctivitis.

In Western medicine, Heal All has always been regarded primarily as a wound herb, giving rise to many of its common names (Woundwort, Wound Root, etc.). Its botanical name, *Prunella*, is derived from *Brunellen*, a name given to it by the Germans, because it rose to prominence when military physicians used it to treat a contagious fever that raged among the German imperial troops in 1547 and 1566, that was characterized by a sore throat and a brown-coated tongue. The fever was called "the browns" (*braun* is the German word for "brown").

In John Gerard's "*Herball*" of 1597, he claimed there was no "better wound herb[e] in the world than Self Heal" (another common name) and said it would "heal any green wound[e]." In 1653, the great English herbalist, Nicholas Culpeper, wrote that "Self Heal" would be good taken both "inwardly or outwardly for wounds and bleeding" and would "cleanse the foulness of sores and speedily heal them."

Seventeenth century herbalist and physician Nicholas Culpepper had observed that when applied on open wounds, self-heal not only impedes the flow of the blood from the wounds, but also repairs the affected area by fusing up the lips of the wounds.

In North America, Heal All's antiseptic and antibacterial effects were said to be particularly good in cases of food poisoning, and in the Pacific Northwest, its juice was used by the Quinault and Quileute tribes for the treatment of boils. They also used the whole plant to treat cuts and inflammations.

Heal All is an astringent, slightly bitter, saline herb that is harvested when in optimum condition (and the plant is in bloom). Although the plant is a member of the mint family, no mint fragrance or flavor is present, and all the aerial (above-ground) parts of the plant are used in herbal medicine. Some of the constituents included in Prunella are volatile oil, a bitter principle, tannin, rutin, beta-carotene, sugar, cellulose and vitamins B-1, C and K.

Life cycle: perennial; herbaceous (Zones 4-9)
Native: Indigenous to Europe and Asia, and practically all temperate regions of the world. Naturalized in parts of N. America as an Eurasian alien.
Height: 6 - 18"
Flower: 1/2"

Heal All is a powerful antiviral, known for its ability to act as a natural "interferon" when dealing with viral infections and to be particularly good in cases of food poisoning.

Heal All is a low growing, spreading, perennial of the mint family. It has very distinctive 'puckered' leaves with an opposite arrangement on square stems. Some burgeoning weed scientists use the 'pruned' texture of the leaves (think about you fingers after swimming) to remember the genus name *Prunella*.

A poultice of self-heal also serves well as a disinfecting agent and is used to pack wounds in the absence of other wound-care material. It was considered by the Chinese to "change the course of a chronic disease". In the traditional Austrian medicine Prunella vulgaris herb has been used internally as tea for treatment of disorders of the respiratory tract and infections.

Heal-All is something of a panacea; it does seem to have some medicinal uses that are constant.

The plants most useful constituents are Betulinic-acid, D-Camphor, Delphinidin, Hyperoside, Manganese, Oleanolic-acid, Rosmarinic-acid, Rutin, Ursolic-acid, and Tannins.

The whole plant is medicinal as alterative, antibacterial, antipyretic, antiseptic, antispasmodic, astringent, carminative, diuretic, febrifuge, hypotensive, stomachic, styptic, tonic, vermifuge and vulnerary.

A cold water infusion of the freshly chopped or dried and powdered leaves is a very tasty and refreshing beverage; weak infusion of the plant is an excellent medicinal eye wash for sties and pinkeye. It is taken internally as a medicinal tea in the treatment of fevers, diarrhea, sore mouth and throat, internal bleeding, and weaknesses of the liver and heart.

Contains the anti-tumor and diuretic compound ursolic acid. Also rich in natural antioxidant compounds, containing more rosmarinic acid than Rosemary.

According to traditional herbalists Deb Jackson and Karen Bergeron writing on Alternative Nature Online Herbal. Modern medical researchers have found that All-Heal has powerful antiviral effects, which may account for the herb's traditional reputation.

The antiviral impact of Prunella vulgaris arises primarily from a nutritive compound called rosmarinic acid, Chinese medical researchers Chuen-lung Cheng and Hongxi Xu report in the "Asian Journal of Traditional Medicines." Extract of P. vulgaris has been successfully used clinically to control gingivitis and to treat aspects of herpes infections, and laboratory studies indicate its potential effectiveness against HIV viruses, according to the journal's report.

Some users who consume Heal All tea have reported a decrease in allergic symptoms, likely related to the anti-inflammatory effects of the herb.

Anti-inflammatory treatments are also usable for many other conditions, and could be implemented to help relieve arthritis or combat other diseases that take advantage of inflamed organs or joints. Although more study is still needed to conclusively determine these health benefits, and users should approach Prunella vulgaris with a level of healthy skepticism, as well as patience as it may take continual usage of tea as part of a dietary plan to feel results.

All-Heal is a powerful tool against allergic responses and has anti-inflammation effects, which may account for these traditional uses. Dr. Ray Sahelian, a practicing physician and medical writer specializing in the use of dietary supplements and natural medicine, reports that at least two laboratory studies reported in peer-review medical journals indicate that Prunella vulgaris inhibits immediate allergic responses and exhibits a strong inhibiting influence on inflammation.

These studies indicate the potential for All-Heal to impart health benefits to allergy sufferers as well as to people with inflammatory ailments like arthritis, although more study is needed to determine the precise mechanisms of these impacts.

Infusion/Tincture: Used to reduce or stop most types of bleeding. One or two teaspoonfuls of crushed and dry self heal herb can be added to one cup of boiling water, and allowed to stand for 10 minutes for proper infusion. The herb itself should not be boiled, alternatively, one or two ml. of self heal tincture may be administered three times daily.

Decoction: Prepared with fresh flower spikes and used to treat high blood pressure, bad temper, anxiety, and hyperactivity. The decoction is frequently mixed with Chinese chrysanthemum (ju hua) for more effective healing.

Poultice: Crushed fresh leaves can be applied directly wounds or used as a dressing for small cuts and scrapes to prevent infection.

Eye and Mouth/Throat Wash: Strain a cup of the infusion through cheese cloth of some other fine filter.

Herb: Used as a preventative measure for many ailments. The flowers, leaves, and tender shoots may be chopped and added to soups, stews, and salads.

Clinical analysis shows it to have an antibacterial action, inhibiting the growth of pseudomonas, Bacillus typhi, E. coli, Mycobacterium tuberculi, which supports its use as an alternative medicine internally and externally as an antibiotic and for hard to heal wounds and diseases. It is showing promise in research for cancer, AIDS, diabetes, and many other maladies.

Folklore: once proclaimed to be a Holy herb and thought to be sent by God to cure all ailments of man or beast, and said to drive away the devil, which lead to the belief that Heal-All was grown in the Witches garden as a disguise. The root was used to make a tea to drink in ceremonies before going hunting by one Native American tribe to sharpen the powers of observation. The Cherokee cooked and ate the young leaves. The Nlaka'pamux drank a cold infusion of the whole plant as a common beverage

The plant contains vitamins A, C, and K, as well as flavonoids and rutin.

Recipe: Medicinal tea or infusion: Add 1 oz. dried or fresh herb to a pint of boiling water, steep till cool, take in cup doses, sweetened with honey, as a general strengthener.

A tea, diluted tincture or fresh plant poultice is effective topically to stop bleeding from cuts or wounds, reduce swelling from insect bites, and to reduce the swelling from varicose veins, hemorrhoids and eye inflammations (sties, conjunctivitis).

Self-heal can be used internally and externally to help dissolve nodules in the neck (such as goiter), lymphomas (fatty tumors).

When Heal All grows to a certain height it will lean, and when it leans far enough the top of the plant attaches itself to the ground and grows new roots into it.

In open and exposed situations, the plant is diminutive, while in more sheltered spots it is larger in all its parts.

If you want to try growing heal-all flowers in your garden you can sow the seeds either in the fall or in the spring. **It is simply too prolific a spreader to be allowed complete freedom to roam the garden.** Many also use the heal-all flower as an ornament. Heal-all is a beautiful flower to use in dried flower decorations.

Cut the flowers in late autumn and hang to dry. You could use them to make beautiful homemade gifts that have not cost you a cent.

By all means, eat some leaves and fresh flower heads if you have access to tender growing specimens. It is good for you. Just add some pieces

to sandwiches or salads.

- This herb is traditionally used in cases of swollen glands and the mumps.
- Many women report it helps release the discomforts of heavy menstrual bleeding.
- It is also diuretic.
- Externally heal-all is used to treat minor wounds. Heal-all tea made from the fresh plant can be used to reduce swelling and stop bleeding of minor wounds.
- Heal-all tea is used as a gargle for sore throats and bleeding gums.

To make the tea use 1-2 teaspoons dried heal-all per cup. Let the infusion sit for about 10 minutes. Finally, Heal All tea benefits also include a direct impact on hyperglycemic conditions. Further studies have shown that the herb helps to regulate insulin and blood sugar levels, assisting with the health of diabetic patients, and potentially alleviating mood swings associated with sugar levels.

I think of the simplest recipe of al is: the "spit poultice." A spit poultice is exactly what it sounds like. Pick a few leaves, chew them up a bit, spit them out, and put them where they're needed. I use spit poultices for bites and stings, scrapes, cuts, bruises, burns, and just about any other mishap my skin might encounter in the summer.

Contraindications:

Currently, there are no known harmful side effects to the use of heal all. Those with diarrhea, nausea, stomachache or vomiting should consult a physician before using Heal Al Herbal Supplement. This herb could potentially interfere with actions of prescription blood thinners (Plavix, Coumadin, etc.)

Man I want A Marigold!
The Common Marigold is familiar to pretty much everyone

Annual
Height: 24 Inches
Bloom Season: Spring/Summer/Fall
Environment: Full Sun/Partial Shade
Zones: All Regions of North America

Calendula **pot marigold (US) or marigold (UK),**

(Calendula officinalis) Hardy annual. Often self-sows.

Whether displaying bright orange or sunny yellow flowers, calendula (also called pot marigold) is one of the most essential parts of your garden medicine chest: Those aromatic flowering heads can be collected and made into oils and salves to help heal skin injuries of all kinds. Make sure you grow only *C. officinalis*, and not any of the many "marigolds" (*Tagetes* spp.) or ornamental varieties that are available. Calendula can grow to almost 2 feet tall, and the flowers tend to open with sunny, dry weather and close in cold or moist conditions.

Harvesting. Collect the flower heads on hot, sunny days for the highest resin content, and pick them regularly to prevent the plants from putting their energy into seed production. Once that happens, the rest of the flowers will be smaller. Choose flowers that are just opening in the morning before 11 a.m. Dry calendula quickly after you harvest it, and check the center of the flower for dryness. Molding in storage is a problem. Watch for reabsorption of moisture, and keep it in complete darkness. Use the entire flower head (not just the petals) in preparations for healing cuts, scrapes, burns, diaper rash, sores, ulcers, varicose veins, chapped skin and lips, and insect bites. Herbalists have long recommended tea infusions of calendula to help heal ulcers in the digestive tract; soothe gallbladder inflammation; and treat enlarged, sore lymph glands.

Preparations and dosage. Use the freshly dried flower heads to make creams, salves, liniments, teas, tinctures, and oils, or add the flower heads directly to your bath to soothe irritated skin. For internal conditions, take 1 to 3 dropperfuls of tincture in a little water several times daily.

Safety. As with other members of the daisy family, some people are sensitive to calendulas because of the sesquiterpene compounds that the plants contain. If you have allergic skin reactions or are sensitive to foods or the environment, start with a low dose of this herb and work up to a full dose, if you don't experience any reaction.

Calendula species have been used traditionally as culinary and medicinal herbs. The petals are edible and can be used fresh in salads or dried and used to color cheese or as a replacement for saffron. A yellow dye has been extracted from the flowers.

The flower petals of the calendula plant (*Calendula officinalis*), or pot marigold, have been used for medicinal purposes since at least the 12th century.

Calendula has high amounts of flavonoids, plant-based antioxidants that protect cells from being damaged by unstable molecules called free radicals. Calendula appears to fight inflammation, viruses, and bacteria. Calendula has been shown to help wounds heal faster, possibly by increasing blood flow and oxygen to the affected area, which helps the body grow new tissue

In some of the earliest medical writings, calendula was recommended for treating ailments of the digestive tract. It was used to detoxify the liver and gall bladder. The flowers were applied to cuts and wounds to stop bleeding, prevent infection and speed healing.

Calendula was also used for various women's ailments, and to treat a number of skin conditions. During the American Civil War, calendula flowers were used on the battlefields in open wounds as antihemorrhagic and antiseptic, and they were used in dressing wounds to promote healing.

Calendula also was used in this way during World War I. Calendula has been historically significant in medicine in many cultures, and it is still important in alternative medicine today. Calendula also has been shown to help prevent dermatitis or skin inflammation in breast cancer patients during radiation therapy. Calendula infusion can be used as an effective douche for treating yeast infections in the vaginal cavity.

Calendula species have been used in cooking for centuries. The flowers were a common ingredient in German soups and stews, which explains the nickname "pot marigold". The lovely golden petals were also used to add color to butter and cheese. The flowers are traditional ingredients in Mediterranean and Middle Eastern dishes.

Culinary uses

The calendula is used in the preparation of many culinary dishes. The addition of fresh and tender calendula leaves to salads and raw vegetable mixtures is an excellent idea. The chopped or whole petals of freshly plucked calendula flowers can also be added to tossed salads to improve the taste.

Calendula floral petals can be used in fresh, dried, or powdered form to impart color and to bring a subtle bittersweet flavor to different foods, including different kinds of sea foods, to chowders and soups, to flavor stews and rice, to add flavor to roast meats and vegetable dishes, or to spice up chicken dishes.

The floral petals of the calendula can be prepared into a flavoring liquid. To make this, the petals of freshly plucked flowers can be chopped and bruised; these should then be soaked in milk or water and left for some time. Once they have been soaked for sometime, the gold colored liquid can be strained and used as required in any dish.

The calendula can act as a substitute in any recipe requiring the use of saffron flowers. Calendula is cheap compared to saffron, the color imparted to the food is of a similar vibrant hue, and however, the flavor imparted to the food is different and equally delicious.

At a commercial level, the flowers of the calendula are employed in coloring poultry products, to color butter and cheese, and as a flavor for ice creams, different soft drinks, baked goods, as well as candy and other condiments.

Craft uses

Calendula is also used in floral displays; the pretty calendula flowers can be included in fresh floral bouquets and arrangements during the summer. The fragrant smelling calendula floral heads and the dried aromatic petals can be included in potpourris and incenses.

Calendula tea provides health benefits, as well as being delicious Calendula flower is used to prevent muscle spasms, start menstrual periods, and reduce fever. It is also used for treating sore throat and mouth, menstrual cramps, cancer, and stomach and duodenal ulcers.

Calendula is applied to the skin to reduce pain and swelling (inflammation) and to treat poorly healing wounds and leg ulcers. It is also applied to the skin (used topically) for nosebleeds, varicose veins, hemorrhoids, inflammation of the rectum (proctitis), and inflammation of the lining of the eyelid (conjunctivitis).

Don't confuse calendula with ornamental marigolds of the Tagets genus, which are commonly grown in vegetable gardens.

Growing. Calendula enjoys full sun—or even partial shade, in hot summer regions—and average soil, and has moderate water needs. If flower production dwindles, you can cut back the plants to increase new flower production. Calendula will self-sow yearly in many gardens, and it doesn't mind crowding. Direct-sow the seed in early spring or late fall, as it can withstand some frost

How effective is it?

Natural Medicines Comprehensive Database rates effectiveness based on scientific evidence according to the following scale: Effective, Likely Effective, Possibly Effective, Possibly Ineffective, Likely Ineffective, Ineffective, and Insufficient Evidence to Rate.

The effectiveness ratings for **CALENDULA** are as follows:

Insufficient evidence to rate effectiveness for...

- **Anal tears (anal fissures)**. Early research suggests that that applying calendula to the affected area may reduce pain in people with anal tears who do not respond to treatment with sitz baths and the medication nifedipine.
- **Diaper rash**. Early research suggests that applying a 1.5% calendula ointment to the skin for 10 days improves diaper rash compared to aloe gel.
- **Ear infections (otitis media)**. Early research shows that applying a specific product (Otikon Otic Solution by Healthy-On Ltd) that contains mullein, garlic, calendula, and St. John's wort to the ear for 3 days reduces ear pain in children and teenagers with ear infections.
- **Skin inflammation due to radiation therapy (radiation dermatitis)**. Early research suggests that applying calendula ointment on the skin might reduce radiation dermatitis in people receiving radiation therapy for breast cancer.
- **Thinning of the wall of the vagina (vaginal atrophy)**. Early research suggests that applying a specific gel (Estromineral Gel, Rottapharm-Madaus) that contains calendula, Lactobacillus sporogenes, isoflavones, and lactic acid to the vagina for 4 weeks reduces symptoms of vaginal atrophy such as vaginal itching, burning, dryness, and pain during intercourse.
- **Leg ulcers**. Early research shows that applying a 7.5% calendula ointment to the skin speeds up the healing of leg ulcers caused by poor blood circulation.
- **Muscle spasms**.
- **Fever**.

- **Cancer**.
- **Nosebleeds**.
- **Varicose veins**.
- **Hemorrhoids**.
- **Promoting menstruation**.
- **Treating mouth and throat soreness**.
- **Wounds**.
- **Other conditions**.

More evidence is needed to rate the effectiveness of calendula for these uses.

Calendula oil is still used medicinally. The oil of *C. officinalis* is used as an anti-inflammatory, an antitumor agent, and a remedy for healing wounds

Allergy to ragweed and related plants: Calendula may cause an allergic reaction in people who are sensitive to the Asteraceae/Compositae family. Members of this family include ragweed, chrysanthemums, marigolds, daisies, and many others. If you have allergies, be sure to check with your healthcare provider before taking calendula.

Sedative medications (CNS depressants)
Calendula might cause sleepiness and drowsiness. Medications that cause sleepiness are called sedatives. Taking calendula along with sedative medications might cause too much sleepiness.

Some sedative medications include clonazepam (Klonopin), lorazepam (Ativan), phenobarbital (Donnatal), zolpidem (Ambien), and others.

Are there interactions with herbs and supplements?

Herbs and supplements that cause sleepiness and drowsiness

Calendula might cause sleepiness and drowsiness. Taking it with other herbs and supplements that have this same effect might cause too much sleepiness. Some of these include 5-HTP, calamus, California poppy, catnip, hops, Jamaican dogwood, kava, St. John's wort, skullcap, valerian, yerba mansa, and others.

Arnica montana (Arnica), used throughout Europe and North America since the 1500's as a cream or ointment, effective for soothing muscles, reducing inflammation and healing wounds.

It is good for back aches. When brewed as a tea, this amazing herb has been used for stress, sleeping problems, emotional trauma making it an excellent "meltdown herb."

Arnica montana is sometimes grown in herb gardens and has long been used medicinally It contains the toxin helenalin, which can be poisonous if large amounts of the plant are eaten. It produces severe gastroenteritis and internal bleeding of the digestive tract if enough material is ingested. Contact with the plant can also cause skin irritation. The roots contain derivatives of thymol, which are used as fungicides and preservatives and may have some anti-inflammatory effect. Arnica cream or oil has long been used externally to treat bruising, soft tissue damage and the shock of impact, whether from falling or being struck. British ambulance crews have long carried arnica to administer to victims of motor vehicle accidents Bruises are reabsorbed more quickly after the use or application of arnica.

Arnica gel is often sold as a homeopathic medicine, in which case the concentration of arnica within it is lower than an undiluted gel. Processed and Prepared Arnica can be purchased at seed and feed stores as horse liniment.

***Actaea racemosa* (Black Cohosh),** a traditional Native American discovery from the root of the cohosh plant known for relieving menstrual cramps and symptoms of menopause such as hot flashes, irritability, mood swings and sleep disturbances. The root of cohosh is an excellent remedy to provide comfort during times of hormonal changes and menstrual periods. It has sedative effects, making it useful for calming nerves, and has been used for assistance during childbirth, which is a particularly high-en Historical use

Native Americans used black cohosh to treat gynecological and other disorders, including sore throats, kidney problems, and depression. Following the arrival of European settlers in the U.S. who continued the medicinal usage of black cohosh, the plant appeared in the U.S. Pharmacopoeia in 1830 under the name "black snakeroot". In 1844 *A. racemosa* gained popularity when Dr. John King, an eclectic physician, used it to treat rheumatism and nervous disorders.

Other eclectic physicians of the mid-nineteenth century used black cohosh for a variety of maladies, including endometritis, amenorrhea, dysmenorrhea, menorrhagia, sterility, severe after-birth pains, and for increased breast milk production.

Contemporary use

Black cohosh is used today mainly as a dietary supplement marketed to women as remedies for the symptoms of premenstrual tension, menopause and other gynecological problems. Recent meta-analysis of contemporary evidence supports these claims. Study design and dosage of black cohosh preparations play a role in clinical outcome, and recent investigations with pure compounds found in black cohosh have identified some beneficial effects of these compounds on physiological pathways underlying age-related disorders like osteoporosis

Side effects

According to Cancer Research UK: "Doctors are worried that using black cohosh long term may cause thickening of the womb lining. This could lead to an increased risk of womb cancer." They also caution that people with liver problems should not take it as it can damage the liver, although a 2011 meta-analysis of research evidence suggested this concern may be unfounded.

Studies on human subjects who were administered two commercially available black cohosh preparations did not detect estrogenic effects on the breast.

Eupatorium perfoliatum (Boneset), an herb traditionally used by Native Americans, who called it "Ague Weed," now commonly called "boneset." Boneset is a traditional natural remedy used by the American Indians in the treatment of a wide range of conditions. These include colds, influenza, rheumatism, dengue (also known as break bone fever, hence the name boneset), malaria and typhoid fever. Native American Indians.

They used it to fight flu and fevers. When they tried to describe the terrible pain that was felt in the bones and the muscles from the fever of influenza, they called it "break bone fever." This fever make you feel like your bones were breaking.

From this name "break bone fever" the name modified to "boneset." It's a great remedy for treating the symptoms of influenza, and helpful for treating aches and pains and fever. Occasional use of boneset leaves brewed as tea helps detoxify the body, removing excess uric acid. It also acts as to expulse other toxins. In a survival instance, this herb can mean the difference between life and death in high fever or poisoning. The Native Americans say the way to overcome sickness, like a cold, the flu, chills and fever, jaundice, sore throat, cholera, malaria or influenza is to sweat. The way to sweat is to drink a lot of hot boneset tea. A fever and sweating is very important to a sick body. That's why the Native Americans had sweat lodges. Sweating helps the body to get rid of poisons through the skin.

Common boneset is native to wetlands and moist lowlands. A far-ranging species found along the edges of streams, lakes and marshes and shores from Canada to Florida and west to Texas and Nebraska. Blooms from June into September. Can grow to five feet in favorable conditions with eight inch leaves. Flowers are white with a blue tinge and grow on heads with ten to forty flowers in each head. As a charm, Native Americans used the root fibers applied to hunting whistles with the belief that they would increase the whistle's ability to call deer.

Boneset has many other names that describe it more clearly. Two of these names are sweat plant and fever wort or fever herb. It is one of the best plants that there is if you have a fever. When you have a dry fever it is like being caught out in the hot desert without any water. You burn up from the outside as well as the inside. In fact, a fever becomes very dangerous when it is a dry fever and the person does not sweat.

That is why another name for this plant is "sweat plant." If you have a dry fever some hot boneset tea will usually cause a person to sweat. When you sweat you cool the body down and you sweat out a lot of toxins. This cools of the body and gets rid a lot of poisons. During the First World War millions of people died from the dreaded influenza. If it were not for the herb boneset, many more would have died. However, many did not know about boneset and many others did not have the faith to use this wonderful herb.

Eupatorium perfoliatum was used in the traditional medicine of Native Americans and extracts are now used in herbal medicine for fever and colds The effects of *Eupatorium perfoliatum* have not been confirmed by clinical study. However, animal studies and *in vitro* experiments with plant extracts indicate possible anti-inflammatory effects and activity against *Plasmodium falciparum*, the parasite that causes malaria

It is also thought that boneset can increase the resistance to infections, loosen phlegm (especially in older patients).

Tiny, white flowers are arranged in fuzzy clusters top the 3-6 ft. stems of this perennial. Hairy plant with dense flat-topped clusters of many dull-white flowers. Paired leaves, united basally, are perforated by the erect stems.

As suggested by the Latin species name, the stem appears to be growing through the leaf. To early herb doctors, this indicated the plant would be useful in setting bones, so its leaves were wrapped with bandages around splints. It is true that very often the names of different plants disclose substantial information regarding them.

However, at times, such information may well be deceptive The Eclectic physician's listed many uses for Boneset, including for "stomach disorders of the inebriate" but here is an important quote "In *influenza* it relieves the pain in the limbs and back. Its popular name, "boneset," is derived from its well-known property of relieving the deep-seated pains in the limbs which accompany this disorder, and *colds* and *rheumatism*".

The reason I include the above quote because a common question is about whether Boneset can be used to mend broken bones, similar to Comfrey. While some herbalists do use it this way, it is more commonly used for viruses. The name boneset is derived from two places. First, the leaves are attached in a way that some people see as a 'doctrine of signatures' suggesting that it can mend broken bones. The second, as in the above quote, is that Boneset has been used for viral infections which are often accompanied by bone and muscle pain, especially during a coughing fit. So by helping stop the virus, Boneset relieves this pain.

For anyone who lives around Boneset, I strongly suggest gathering a good amount of the leaves and unopened flower heads when you have the chance. They dry pretty easy and are helpful for respiratory viruses. They are also useful as a diaphoretic, to help bring on suppressed fever. (It is important to know when to break a fever versus when to suppress it).

Eclectic medical practitioners have also reported that they have employed boneset in the form of an effectual defensive as well as curative for the 'Spanish influenza' outbreak in 1918, in addition to flu pandemics during the 19th century.

Boneset is easily identified apart from the Joe pye weeds (and most other plants) by the way the leaves are joined together around the stem.

In general, E. purpureum, a species related to boneset and universally called joe-pye weed shares the therapeutic attributes possessed by boneset. Joe-pye weed can be recognized by its purple hued blooms. This species derives its name from an Indian medicine practitioner.

In fact, this Indian medicine practitioner, who was reputed throughout New England for using this herb to treat typhus, has been honored by using his name to classify joe-pye weed. Nevertheless, majority of people who are authorities in herbal medicine, believe that compared to boneset, joe-pye weed (E. purpureum) is less effective in curing fevers.

Boneset-Perfoliate Leaves

This common wetland plant has a long rich history of medicinal use both in past and current practice. The leaves and flowers are taken as a tea or tincture, though it is quite bitter tasting. It is one of my favorite herbs for colds and influenza. It is relatively safe and a few good strong cups of the infusion or a dropperful or two of tincture every few hours can speed up the rate of recovery. Best to take it as soon as you feel the virus coming on (which is generally true for most medicines).

The dried leaves have also been used to make a tonic, boneset tea, thought effective in treating colds, coughs, and constipation. Mature specimens will slowly spread in gardens by means of rhizomes to form large clumps and small colonies. It will provide a visually stunning background in any moist, cottage garden or perennial flower bed. Blooms in mid-summer through mid-fall: July to October. Very cold hardy: zones 3-8

Propagation

Propagate from seed. Germination of stored seeds will be facilitated by a 3 week period of cold stratification. Mature clumps can be divided in early spring or late fall. Early summer soft wood cuttings may also be successful.

Habitat

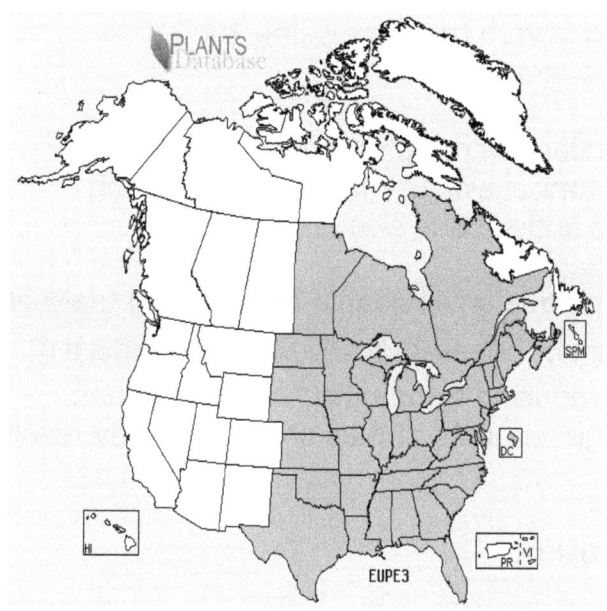

Boneset is mainly found in the temperate regions of North America, ranging from Florida to Canada. It is found as far west as Texas and is a common weed along the edges of swamps and along streams. It has a high affinity for moisture and prefers wet ground.

Additionally it has been used as an herbal folk medicine for fibromyalgia, diarrhea and intestinal worms.

Some studies done on animals indicate that boneset does in fact have the ability to reduce the symptoms of arthritis and malaria. While few clinical trials have been done, there is anecdotal evidence of this in humans.

Boneset is thought to reduce fevers by increased sweating. Known as "Bone-set", from the prompt manner in which it relieves pain in limbs and muscles that accompanies some forms of febrile disease, like malaria and influenza. One point to keep in mind is that the more general and severe the bone pains, the better adapted is the case of this remedy.

Boneset has anti-inflammatory properties that make it a useful herbal remedy for topical skin irritants. It is also being studied in its ability to aid and subdue skin diseases.

Compared with aspirin, a small double-blind clinical trial of a homeopathic preparation of boneset (N=53) found the herbal treatment as effective in reducing symptoms of the common cold. The ingestion of large amounts of teas or extracts may result in severe diarrhea. http://www.drugs.com/npp/boneset.html - ref14

Dosage and Administration

The mode of administration of boneset depends on the condition for which is being taken. The traditional means are as a tincture or a tea.

It is thought that a hot tea is best for the treatment of colds and fevers, even though it does have a bitter taste. Teas are made by adding boiling water to approximately 1 to 2 grams of the herb (about 1/2 teaspoon). This is allowed to steep for a maximum of 15 minutes and then drunk. Three cups a day should not be exceeded.

The tincture is best used as a tonic or laxative. It should be taken thirty minutes before meals and 4 ml. (3/4 teaspoon) three times a day is the recommended dosage.

The plant does contain minimal amounts of potentially liver-harming pyrrolizidine alkaloids so overdosing should be avoided.

Knows chill is coming on because he cannot drink enough. Perspiration relieves all symptoms except headache

There is no recent clinical evidence to guide dosage of boneset. Traditional use was at a dose of 2 g of leaves and flowers. Internal use should be tempered by the occurrence of hepatotoxic pyrrolizidine alkaloids in this plant.

The attic, or woodshed, of almost every country farm-house has its bunches of the dried herb hanging tops downward from the rafters during the whole year, ready for immediate use should some member of the family, or that of a neighbor, be taken with a cold. "How many children have winced when the maternal edict, `drink this boneset; it'll do you good,' has been issued; and how many old men have craned their necks to allow the nauseous dose the quicker to pass the palate!" Eupatorium perf. was first proved by Drs. Williamson and Neidhard in 1846.

Potential Side Effects of Boneset

Boneset is fairly free of major side effects. The herb does not have the best taste in the world and, as such, some cases of nausea or vomiting have been reported. It is thought that the dried herb causes less of a reaction than the fresh plant so this is an option for those experiencing such symptoms. This infusion is given in the hot form to reduce fevers, while the cold infusion is effective as a tonic. Boneset is an effective medication for treating catarrh (inflammation of the mucus membrane, particularly of the respiratory tract), especially when one is suffering from influenza. In fact, the infusion prepared with boneset has been employed widely and with the best endeavours - often given warm in measures of a wineglass at intervals of 30 minutes, while the patient is bed ridden all the time. When the medication has been given four to five dosages, abundant sweating occurs and the patient feels relieved. As mentioned before, it has been said that the common name of the herb, boneset, has been derived from the effectiveness of this herb in curing influenza, which was prevalent in the United States at one point of time.

While the plant only contains trace amounts of pyrrolizidine alkaloids, those who are suffering from liver disease should not use it. Others who should avoid the use of boneset include women who are pregnant and breast-feeding.

No one should use boneset for longer than six months at a time. Speaking to a health care provider is recommended before considering trying this herb as a natural remedy for any condition.

The source of the common name of boneset is not clear. One proposition is that dengue fever (a mosquito-transmitted viral infection marked by muscle and bone pain), formally known as breakbone fever, was relieved by boneset (Innvista 2007). Another suggests that boneset is used by indigenous people to heal broken bones (Innvista 2007). In the early years of medicine, *Eupatorium perfoliatum* was placed on bandages of broken bones. The rationale behind this therapy was one of Doctrine of Signatures. The users believed that the jointed appearance of the leaves was an indication that this plant healed broken bones (Connecticut Botanical Society 2005). Boneset has also been shown to help treat wounds, cuts and other skin problems (Dweck 1997). In conclusion, the scant research conducted to date suggest that boneset may have many beneficial effects such as fighting off cold and flu, treating malaria, boosting the immune system, and may have some effect on reducing tumors.

Times of India News - Plant for Dengue   Dt. 13 Nov 2012

The King Institute team headed by a Chennai-based homoeopath administered the drug extracted from Eupatorium perfoliatum to 50 patients with secondary dengue and found all of them recovered. "The platelet counts came under control for almost all patients and blood tests showed marked improvement," said King Institute director Dr P Gunasekaran. The study, lead by Dr N R Jayakumar of Madan Homoeo Clinic, was presented at an international symposium on 'Challenges and strategies in the prevention and management of viral infections' at Central Learther Research Institute recently.

Jayakumar said it wasn't a new idea to administer the drug to patients with dengue. Earlier the drug was given to patients in Delhi and Sri Lanka during epidemics. In June, the drug was administered to dengue patients at the Madurai Government Rajaji Hospitals. "We wanted to scientifically prove the drug is efficient. The patients were given two doses a day. The platelet count of all the patients improved. The good thing about this drug is that it can also be given alongside allopathic medicines," Dr Jayakumar said.

"In allopathic medicine, there is no drug for this disease. The only treatment is IV fluids to replace body fluids. Most patients we chose for the study had platelet count less than 10,000. We prevented death and blood transfusion in all the 50 patients who took this drug," said Dr Gunasekaran.

Dengue virus is spread by aedes mosquito. The symptoms include fever, headache, body pain and rashes. Some patients develop life-threatening dengue hemorrhagic fever, resulting in bleeding, low levels of blood platelets and blood plasma leakage.

Usual dosage

Boneset is taken in the form of an infusion as well as a tincture.

Infusion: To prepare a boneset infusion, add one to two teaspoonfuls of the dehydrated herb to a cup (250 ml) of boiling water and allow it to permeate for about 10 to 15 minutes. For best results, drink this infusion as hot as you can. The infusion should be drunk at intervals of 30 minutes to treat flu or any other type of fevers.

Tincture: For optimum results, the boneset tincture should be taken in dosages of 2 ml to 4 ml at least thrice every day.

ounce to a pint of boiling water was used to treat dengue or "breakbone fever". Used by Midwestern Native Americans as a tea to help break a fever and treat bronchitis, sore throats and colds. It is also reported to be a laxative or stimulant in smaller doses. Boneset is also used to treat influenza, swine flu, acute bronchitis, nasal inflammation, joint pain (rheumatism), fluid retention, dengue fever, and pneumonia; as a stimulant; and to cause sweating.

Eupatorium perfoliatum is a moisture loving plant. The nectar rich flowers will attract a great variety of pollinators. The bitter leaves tend do deter herbivores from browsing them. All parts of the plant should be considered toxic if ingested in large quantities. According to the USDA: "The leaves have been used to treat dengue fever. Modern German research suggests that common boneset may act as a general immune system stimulant". It has traditionally been used as a weak anti-inflammatory and laxative.

When taken in reasonable measures, boneset is considered to be a gentle stimulant, in addition to being a diaphoretic (an agent that encourages sweating), particularly when it is taken in the form of a warm infusion. Warm boneset infusion is also taken to cure muscular spasms in rheumatic attacks. When taken in large amounts, boneset is emetic (a medical agent that causes vomiting) as well as a laxative.

4) **Calendula officinalis** (Calendula), is one of the most widely used herbs for relieving an upset stomach, ulcers, menstrual cramps and is known for having anti-inflammatory, antiviral and antibacterial effects. A boutique soap and cosmetic maker charges upwards of $40 per bottle of skin toner made from calendula extract. You can make this at home. The most helpful use of calendula is as a tincture made from leaves or flowers, used as soak for poultices to help heal wounds. It is a great, natural antibacterial agent.

A PREPPERS HERBAL

5) ***Nepeta cataria*** (Catnip), has a long history of being used as a digestive aid. It's a natural sedative that also helps to ease digestion, colic and diarrhea. Dehydration caused by diarrhea, and high body temperatures caused by fevers can be life-threatening. A tea brewed from its leaves may help alleviate these symptoms. Catnip is also a mild sedative that naturally helps calm the nerves during stressful situations.

6) ***Capsicum annuum*** (Red Pepper), is a powerful pain reliever when applied topically, and is used to treat osteoarthritis and rheumatoid arthritis and shingles. Use this pepper to help with everything from seasickness to a fever. It is easy to grow, and versatile in use, which means it should be a staple of your survival medicine cabinet.

7) ***Anthemis nobilis*** (Chamomile), one of the oldest and favorites in any herb garden for its soothing power and calming effect is also known to prevent nightmares. Use a tea brewed from the leaves and flowers of chamomile to help ease stress-- including anxiety and panic attacks. The detoxifying and anti-anxiety benefits make this easy-to-grow herb a must-have. It promotes overall health and strength.

8) ***Cichorium intybus*** (Chicory Root), was traditionally used as an additive to coffee, or as a substitute for coffee. It's a natural

sedative and anti-inflammatory that treats jaundice, helps the body resist gallstones and liver stones, and aids in reducing the levels of LDL cholesterol in the blood. This herb is particularly useful to rid the body of parasites, which are held mostly at bay by modern medicine. The flowers, used as a poultice, help with wound healing.

9) **Symphytum officinale** (Comfrey), a great first aid for external treatment for wounds and to reduce inflammation associated with sprains and broken bones. Keeps this herb growing in the garden so it is readily available for external salves and poultices to help broken bones heal faster. (The plant can also be tilled back into the soil as a natural fertilizer, as it contains high levels of nitrogen in its tissue.)

A PREPPERS HERBAL

10) ***Echinacea purpurea*** (Purple Coneflower), is one of the most popular herbal medicines today. It has been used for more than 400 years to treat infections, wounds, even malaria, blood poisoning and diphtheria. Drinking tea from Echinacea helps the body regain strength, and helps rid the body of the common cold up to three times faster than doing nothing. Growing your own is a perfect alternative to paying for expensive over-the-counter remedies.

11) ***Oenothera biennis*** (Evening Primrose), is great for eczema, dermatitis and skin allergies. It can also reduce inflammations,

ease bloating of menstrual discomfort, and strengthens liver functions. One of the most interesting uses of evening primrose is to help alleviate symptoms of multiple sclerosis and other nerve disorders. It is one of the few herbs that can help with nerve problems.

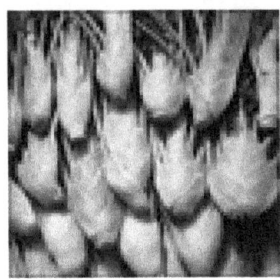

12) **Foeniculum vulgare** (Fennel), used by the Chinese for centuries to treat hernia, indigestion and abdominal pain. Adding fennel to tea or to a recipe that could cause digestive upset can prevent the digestive upset. Tea brewed from the fennel plant alleviates chronic coughs. It can also act as a cough syrup and an expectorant to help clear mucus from the lungs. Oil of fennel can be used as an external pain reliever for sore muscles.

13) **_Tanacetum parthenium_** (Feverfew),
native to southeastern Europe, feverfew is now widespread throughout Europe, North America, and Australia. The migraine-relieving activity of feverfew is believed to be due to parthenolide, an active compound that helps relieve smooth muscle spasms. In particular, it helps prevent the constriction of blood vessels in the brain (one of the leading causes of migraine headaches). Medicinally use the feverfew leaves, but all parts of the plant that grow above ground may also be used for medicinal purposes.

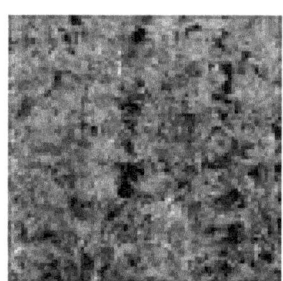

14) **_Hyssopus officinalis_** (Hyssop), mentioned in the Bible, is an

excellent expectorant and stimulant. It is also frequently used for relief of muscular rheumatism, for bruises and contusions. Tea made from the flowers of this herb is good to have on hand for people needing assistance with breathing problems. It has positive affects on the lungs, and can be helpful for asthmatics.

15) **Lavandula officinalis** (Lavender), is popular in soaps, shampoos and fragrances, but is also a natural remedy for insomnia, anxiety, depression and is known for its soothing effect. Never use lavender on an open wound, but otherwise it is an excellent and soothing herb. It is one of the few herbs that helps combat hair loss. Essentials from the lavender plant have natural anti-depressant properties when used aromatically.

A PREPPERS HERBAL

16) **Melissa officinalis** (Lemon Balm), a member of the mint family, is used to help treat sleep disorders when brewed as a tea. Potentially, the most useful application of lemon balm in the realm of the home is that oils from the lemon balm plant are a natural mosquito repellant. It can be rubbed on the body as a repellent. This helps aid in comfort, but also helps to repel mosquitoes that carry infectious disease.

17) **Althaea officinalis** (Marshmallow), the root of this plant traditionally used to treat asthma, bronchitis, sore throat, cough and even the common cold. It aids in production of milk for mothers who breast feed. In emergency situations, this plant has medicinal properties that help dissolve kidney stones and improve kidney functions, when a tea made by boiling the root is consumed. The roots, when boiled with onions, are also an emergency food source.

18) **Valarian officinalis** (Valerian), has been used as far back as the 2nd century A.D. to treat insomnia, anxiety, nervousness, seizures and epilepsy. Valerian is a natural anti-anxiety remedy. It is also useful for treating headaches, even migraines. A definite must for the herbal remedy garden.

19) **Achillea millefolium** (Yarrow), named after Achilles who had used this medicinal to stop the bleeding wounds of his soldiers. Used today to treat minor bleeding, inflammation fever and infection. Use this herb topically to ease discomfort of hemorrhoids, stop bleeding, as an anti-inflammatory to ease swelling. Tea brewed from the flowers and leaves will help stop diarrhea, and its potential disastrous dehydrating effects, and helps purge the body of bacterial infections.

20) **Rosmarinus officinalis** (Rosemary), used for indigestion, to treat muscle pain and arthritis, and to improve circulation. Tea brewed from the leaves and taken internally can slow brain degeneration due to Alzheimer's disease. It can also counteract nerve degeneration due to Lou Gehrig's disease.

Disclaimer: Statements contained herein have not been evaluated by the Food and Drug Administration. These products are not intended to diagnose, treat and cure or prevent disease.

This intended as a reference volume only, not as a medical manual. The information given here is designed to help you make informed decisions about your health. It is not intended as a substitute for any treatment that may have been prescribed by your doctor. If you suspect that you have a medical problem, we urge you to seek competent medical help.

Feed yourself for free:

Dandelion (*Taraxacum officinale*)

Compared with an equal weight of lettuce, dandelion has three times the vitamin C, four times the protein, carbohydrate, fat, calcium, iron and vitamin B, five times the phosphorous - and an astounding 12 times the vitamin A. After that shopping list, it's almost surprising to hear it's good to eat as well.

Its leaves and roots are available the year round although, like all greens, the young leaves gathered in the spring make the best eating.

You can spur its leaf production, by cutting off the flower heads before they unfurl and, in winter, by covering the plant with a flowerpot and sacking, or otherwise protecting from frost.

Dandelion is one of the few welcome exceptions to the golden rule that... wild plants which exclude a milky sap when cut, are best left alone.

Comfrey (*Symphytum officinale*)

The broad fleshy leaves of comfrey feel the way a hairbrush looks, but the disquieting furriness quite disappears, like that of nettles, in cooking. Renowned by herbalists as a 'miracle' healing plant that, in a poultice, quickly sets bones and reduces swellings, sprains and bruises, comfrey also has good value.

Caution: Comfrey, like bracken tops, is said to be potentially carcinogenic, if consumed over time in vast quantities. (As, of course, is tobacco.) This thought may not concern you overmuch in a survival situation but in normal times all herbs should be used in sensible moderation.

Nutritionally, comfrey is equal to most fodder plants, but per plant is more abundant in leaf than many, and can be picked the year round. Seek it out by ditches, riverbanks and other damp places. Either young or old leaves may be eaten, plus the stems and flowers, for comfrey is rarely as bitter as many 'weeds.' But for the best flavor, use the young leaves or blanch the plant for a few weeks by covering it with earth.

Comfrey has more mucilage (thick gooey substance) than even marshmallow, so its roots and leaves are excellent, dried and stored, as a 'flour' which can be mixed with wheat flour (or equal parts of soy and wheat flour) plus water to make pastry, intriguingly green but nutritious. It will also bind together croquettes and patties, in the absence of egg - a valuable economy tip. It will thicken sauces and fortify stews. The very young mucilaginous leaves, deep-fry (as do wild mallow leaves), particularly well in tempura.

Comfrey cakes are a tasty way to use leftover. Steam or simmer washed leaves for five minutes or until soft, then chop and sauté them briskly with onions. Mix with an equal amount of mashed cooked pulses, grains, rice or potato. Add some herbs and a dash of Worcester sauce and form into cakes. Bake or grill for about 15 minutes until brown on both sides.

Use comfrey leaves in a casserole as the layers or use as a side dish to meat or sausages by quickly sautéing in butter.

Sorrel (*Rumex acetosa*)

This is one of the easiest herbs to spot. Its rusty brown seed spike thrusts conspicuously from every motorway verge and acid city soil from summer through to spring. And it's no matter if its seed head and long spear-shaped leaves should be confused with the very similar spike but broader leaves of dock, its near cousin. Dock is edible, although formidably bitter.

Sorrel is high in vitamins A and C, and many minerals, especially iron. But the oxalic acid - which provides its sour taste and the brown blotches on older leaves - can be harmful to rheumatics and other sufferers from over-acidity.

This tartness can be exploited for its own sake in sharp sauces, e.g. for fish dishes, or can be removed by boiling for 20 minutes in two lots of water (or you may need at least three, if you've picked dock by mistake.) Or it can be offset by combining sorrel with bland greens, like comfrey, nettle, plantain, spinach and so on; or with sweet tubers like parsnip and beet.

It is best gathered in spring and can either be dried in bulk to reconstitute for purees, drinks or sauces during the year, or may be used fresh, e.g. chopped raw as a flavoring herb to scatter on salads, cheese dishes or soup. It can also be used in quiche or in a Mornay sauce, made of cheese, cream and white wine.

Yarrow (*Achillea millefolium*)

The feathery leaves of yarrow look like an unpromising food, and their bitter spicy taste and aroma would seem to confirm this. Yet you can count on yarrow, along with plantain and dandelion, to be profusely available in the sootiest depths of the city on the worst soil the year round.

It rates high on minerals, particularly copper and will itself supply an entire pharmacy of herbal remedies, when either eaten raw or infused with tea. To eat, the older leaves should be very well chopped or else have their fibrous spine stripped off.

Add the nutritious leaves or tiny white flowers finely shredded to salads of cucumber and cooked potato, with a dressing of vinaigrette (or mayonnaise, cream, or lemon juice sweetened with honey). Mix them with grated raw carrot and beetroot, which themselves are often sweet enough to offset any bitterness. Scatter them, dried and powdered or freshly chopped, on sandwich spreads or in sweet desserts or drinks.

Yarrow is abundant enough to collect in bulk. Boil it for 20 minutes in two changes of water, to eat as a vegetable - either on its own tossed in butter or with bland vegetables like comfrey or fat hen.

Creamed yarrow is (if you use the youngest leaves) a very pleasant dish. Beat two eggs with 4oz (113g) of honey and four tablespoons of vinegar (preferably cider vinegar). Add a knob of melted butter, season and heat gently until boiling. Stir in a cupful of cream and mix all with the cooked yarrow to form a thick creamy serving. It can be eaten as it is or used as a filling for pies, pastries or homemade ravioli.

Stinging Nettle (*Urtica dioica*)

Every child soon becomes familiar with nettles. Their antidote is usually a much later discovery. Either cooking or drying the plant, however, banishes both their disconcerting hairs and their sting - which is ammonium bicarbonate and harmless. (Incidentally, its remedy is the juice of dock, sage, mint, rosemary or even nettle itself.)

These processes turn nettle into perhaps the most valuable of the survival herbs. Nettles are abundant, especially on rubbish heaps and they hold major amounts of vitamin C (more than spinach,) of protein (5.5%,) and of nearly all the minerals a human needs and notably iron and phosphorus.

Dried and powdered, they are therefore invaluable as a daily food supplement throughout the winter months, perhaps kept in the shaker as a salt substitute (safer for diabetics or those on a sodium-free diet.) The young leaves at any season are palatable, although you will harvest the best crop in spring for drying and should remove the coarser stems before cooking. The old leaves are not only very astringent in taste, but eaten in excess can cause kidney damage.

Add chopped nettles to any green vegetable, stew or soup, or juice them with others in a vegetable cocktail.

The Scottish nettle pudding is of historic vintage and is easily prepared : Mix one part by weight of cooked pureed young nettles with one part together of equal weights of cabbage (or Brussels sprouts,) onions (or leeks,) part-cooked grains, plus some rashers of fried bacon, a sprinkle of herbs, seasoning and an optional beaten egg.

Moisten with stock, tie in muslin in a pudding basin and cook in a medium oven for one and a half hours, or 30 minutes in a pressure cooker.

Food for free: The last three in our series of the 12 'Survival Plants' that can provide us with all the nutrients we need.

Chickweed (*Stellaria media*)

Although often more prominent in January than August, the fragile-looking chickweed plagues gardeners at any time. But its succulent sweet leaves hold ample minerals - especially copper and iron - and they are the equal of watercress in both vitamins and (with suitable preparation) flavor. Gather vast quantities, for it reduces dramatically during cooking.

To guarantee winter supplies, cover a promising bed with dry leaves from October on.

Cook washed leaves for just two minutes in minimum water and add nutmeg, chopped onion greens and chives and a squeeze of lemon. This can be used as a bed for game, poultry or rich meat.

It is excellent raw in salads and can offset tartness of dandelion or sorrel. For a colorful buffet dish, mix them with whole nuts; sliced apple (sprinkled with lemon juice to retard discoloring,) chopped raw cauliflower and orange segments.

Plantain (*Plantago major*)

In common with chamomile and grass, plantain seems to thrive for being walked on and luxuriates throughout even winter months by city paths. It is high in minerals, plus vitamin C and K and a factor said to check bleeding.

It is not only a perennial 'anti-scurvy' vegetable, but its juice also gives year-round first aid for small wounds and soothes insect bites or stings. 'Wild food' guides disdain it because its ribbed spear or shield shaped leaves are fibrous and tough. But for its convenience as a hoard of important nutrients within continual reach of any city dweller, it amply repays acquaintance - and a little care in its cooking.

Grass (*Poa annua* etc.)

We unlike cows and such are not built to digest grass but chewing on it and swallowing the juice can be beneficial. Most of us have chewed a grass stem at some time. But you have only to suggest that grass, with simple preparation, can be made a nutritious everyday food suitable for human consumption, for your audience to edge - and to become suspiciously agreeable.

Yet common lawn grass is more nourishing than virtually any other green vegetable. It contains every vitamin, mineral and other nutrient essential to health, with the exceptions of vitamins D and B12 (which are claimed, somewhat controversially, to be synthesizable by the body itself under special conditions.)

When dried, grass contains nearly half its weight in protein (i.e. three times the protein of prime beef,) and a mere 15lb (6.8kg) of dried grass is said to contain the nutrient content of 350lb (159kg) of other fresh vegetables.

Today it's smuggled in to convalescent food supplements, chlorophyll tablets and toothpaste. Grass is a survival food. It's ubiquitous, sustaining - but universally unsuspected.

Grass can be made into chlorophyll biscuits or juice.

Chlorophyll biscuits: Into 8oz (227g) of wheat or barley flour, rub 1oz (28g) of fat or oil and one teaspoon of salt. When amalgamated, add powdered grass to make up 25% of the volume, plus enough liquid (ideally, milk or vegetable cooking water) to make dough. Beat the dough for 10 minutes with a rolling pin and roll into small pieces, as thin as possible. Prick all over and bake for five minutes in a very hot oven or until the edges are brown.

Brown food coloring can be added to hide the green tinge.

. Groundnut: The American groundnut (Apios americana), also called the Indian potato, is one of those perennial vegetables that doesn't get much attention, but could be a great addition to any garden. The groundnut is a perennial vine that produces edible beans and large edible tubers (more properly "rhizomatous stems"), and is native to the eastern portion of the US. The vines grow to about six feet long, and can be grown up a trellis (or up other plants) for dense plantings. The groundnuts are harvested in the fall, and as with sunchokes, some should be left in the ground for next year's growth.

Storing Seeds

Storing survival seeds is easy, takes up little space and they truly are insurance no company can provide you with.

The best way to store seeds is to package them in paper envelopes or bags since they allow for good air circulation and don't sweat. Keep in mind that humidity and lack of air circulation will cause mold, disease and prompt seeds to germinate prematurely.

There are no shortages of websites out there selling survival seeds and the vast majority of them are selling vegetable and herb seeds. Many are heirloom or non-GMO and some are just basic seeds. The marketing on these are quite amazing as many companies offer packages. Some of these packages are "plant a full acre," "non-hybrid gift variety," "wholesale bulk," "doomsday preppers," and the list goes on.

Let's look at this logically. On one hand having seeds to grow a garden is smart however, trying to grow a vegetable garden will be very challenging if there is little or no rain. Relying on tap water may also not be possible if restrictions are implemented.

All is not doom and gloom here. Yes, purchase and save vegetable seeds, but more importantly save seeds from edible wild plants. Weeds grow in the most inhospitable of conditions therefore making them more reliable than cultivated food. Growing weeds in your backyard is as simple as tossing the seeds onto the ground.

Weed Seeds Last Longer

It is truly incredible how long (wild edible) seeds last. In fact, many wild edible seeds last up to 40 years (in the soil) before they germinate. Mullein seeds can survive up to 100 years, and each plant produces 22,300 seeds.

Curly dock (yellow dock) seeds last up to 80 years and each plant produces 29,500 seeds. Purslane, pigweed and lamb's quarters 'seeds last up to 40 years, meanwhile chickweed and mustards can last up to 10 years.

The dandelion seed can last up to 6 years and each dandelion plant produces up to 15,000 seeds.

Check out how many seeds one plant produces:

- Purslane: 52,300
- Lamb's quarters: 72,450
- Pigweed: 117,400

All of these plants are edible and between the dandelion, alfalfa, lamb's quarters, purslane and pigweed you get every mineral, vitamin, protein, Omega's and other essential nutrients your body needs to survive and survive healthy!

Seeds are perfect for collecting right now in many areas of the northern hemisphere. It doesn't take long to go out and collect seeds and the best part of all you get fresh air and exercise.

Start saving seeds today – because we don't know what tomorrow may bring.

Clovers *(Trifolium)*

Lucky you-clovers are actually edible. And they're found just about everywhere there's an open grassy area. You can spot them by their distinctive trefoil leaflets. You can eat clovers raw, but they taste better boiled.

Wood Sorrel (*Oxalis*)

You'll find wood sorrel in all parts of the world; species diversity is particularly rich in South America. Humans have used wood sorrel for food and medicine for millennia. The Kiowa Indians chewed on wood sorrel to alleviate thirst, and the Cherokee ate the plant to cure mouth sores. The leaves are a great source of vitamin C.

The roots of the wood sorrel can be boiled.
They're starchy and taste a bit like a potato.

Purslane *(Portulaca oleracea)*

    While considered an obnoxious weed in the United States, purslane can provide much needed vitamins and minerals in a wilderness survival situation. Ghandi actually numbered purslane among his favorite foods. It's a small plant with smooth fat leaves that have a refreshingly sour taste. Purslane grows from the beginning of summer to the start of fall. You can eat purslane raw or boiled. If you'd like to remove the sour taste, boil the leaves before eating.

Plantain (*Plantago*)

Found in all parts of the world, the plantain plant (not to be confused with the banana-like plantain) has been used for millennia by humans as a food and herbal remedy for all sorts of maladies. You can usually find plantains in wet areas like marshes and bogs, but they'll also sprout up in alpine areas. The oval, ribbed, short-stemmed leaves tend to hug the ground. The leaves may grow up to about 6" long and 4" wide. It's best to eat the leaves when they're young. Like most plants, the leaves tend to get bitter tasting as they mature. Plantain is very high in vitamin A and calcium. It also provides a bit of vitamin C.

Chickweed *(Stellaria media)*

You'll find this herb in temperate and arctic zones. The leaves are pretty hefty, and you'll often find small white flowers on the plant. They usually appear between May and July. You can eat the leaves raw or boiled. They're high in vitamins and minerals.

Curled Dock *(Rumex crispus)*

You can find curled dock in Europe, North America, South America, and Australia. It's distinguished by a long, bright red stalk that can reach heights of three feet. You can eat the stalk raw or boiled. Just peel off the outer layers first. It's recommend that you boil the leaves with several changes of water in order to remove its naturally bitter taste.

Dandelion *(Taraxacum officinale)*

Compared with an equal weight of lettuce, dandelion has three times the vitamin C, four times the protein, carbohydrate, fat, calcium, iron and vitamin B, five times the phosphorous - and an astounding 12 times the vitamin A. After that shopping list, it's almost surprising to hear it's good to eat as well.

Its leaves and roots are available the year round although, like all greens, the young leaves gathered in the spring make the best eating.

You can spur its leaf production, by cutting off the flower heads before they unfurl and, in winter, by covering the plant with a flowerpot and sacking, or otherwise protecting from frost.

Dandelion is one of the few welcome exceptions to the golden rule that... wild plants which exclude a milky sap when cut, are best left alone.

Sure, it's an obnoxious weed on your perfectly mowed lawn, but when you're out in the wild this little plant can save your life. The entire plant is edible- roots, leaves, and flower. Eat the leaves while they're still young; mature leaves taste bitter. If you do decide to eat the mature leaves, boil them first to remove their bitter taste. Boil the roots before eating as well. You can drink the water you boiled the roots in as a tea and use the flower as a garnish for your dandelion salad.

The above list represents just an introductory glance at what these powerful and easy to grow herbs can do to keep you in top shape. You should research and record all the beneficial effects of common herbs that you can grow in your garden so that you will have your own home-grown pharmacy in times of emergency.

Also, be sure to invest time in researching herbal combinations. Often the power of herbal medicine can be multiplied by combining complimentary herbs to build a much more effective remedy from the combination as compared to the effects of the individual herbs.

A PREPPERS HERBAL

Garden tower that uses the principle of Vermicultture Project for your yard and garden (yarden?).

Vermiculture Worm Tower

Would you like to eliminate several steps in composting?

Vermicomposting or Worm Poo

The reason earthworms are essential for healthy soil is because they wiggle around the soil helping to aerate it, but the best quality of the earthworm is its poo (or castings). The castings not only provide valuable nutrients to the soil, but the poo also contains beneficial microorganisms from the earthworm's digestive system. Beneficial microorganisms are vital for breaking down organic matter into a form that plant roots can intake.

Vermicomposting is the farming of worms in order to collect their castings to use as a fertilizer or top dressing. You can also purchase worm castings and earthworm cocoons to place in raised beds or large containers. The cocoons will hatch earthworms introducing these soil soldiers to your vegetable garden.

A Worm Tower is basically a length of pipe buried halfway in the ground with holes drilled in the buried part for worms to get in and out. Food scraps are added directly to the tower instead of your composting bin, and are eaten by worms already living in the target part of your yard. You can add Worm Towers to your full blown vermiculture / vermicomposting regime or just use them by themselves.

I like this for the same reason I like precycling; several steps and lots of time can be eliminated for some of your composting by just delivering food waste directly to the worms, directly to the garden.

A worm tower is a simple and effective way to take any garden bed from average yield to gloriously abundant.

Essentially a worm tower is an in-garden worm farm that allows the worms and their nutrients to interact directly with the surrounding garden bed. It consists of a vertical pipe, placed half-submerged in a garden bed, with holes drilled in it.

The idea is basically to put a simple worm farm directly into your raised garden bed. Essentially a worm tower is an in-garden worm farm that allows the worms and their nutrients to interact directly with the surrounding garden bed. It consists of a vertical pipe, placed half-submerged in a garden bed, with holes drilled in it.

And though you do need to keep feeding them, a worm tower is an incredibly effective and low energy-input way of increasing the goodness in your garden, and they're very easy to get going and to maintain.

To make your own worm tower, you will need:

1. A piece of wide plastic pipe (150mm wide or thereabouts) about 50cm long.
2. A drill, to make holes in the pipe
3. A saw, to cut the pipe to your desired length
4. Compost worms! 50 would be plenty
5. Newspaper and water

6. A terracotta pot (or similar) to fit over the end of the pipe

☐ Add a thick layer of dry carbon material (straw, dry grass etc) in the bottom of the pipe, to a depth of 10cm
☐ Tear your newspaper into strips and soak in a bucket of water (or use some other carbon-rich material for this step – straw, dead grass, etc).
☐ Place a thick bedding of wet newspaper strips in the bottom of the pipe, maybe 15cm deep.
☐ Add your worms!
☐ Add another layer (5cm) of wet newspaper to bed the worms down, and help them get over the excitement of becoming worm tower residents.

Benefits of Vermicomposting:

- Improves the physical structure of the soil
- Enriches soil with micro-organisms
- Improves water holding capacity
- Enhances germination, plant growth, and crop yield
- Improves root growth and structure
- Reduces amount of waste going to landfills
- Microbial activity in worm castings is 10 to 20 times higher than in the soil and organic matter that the worm ingests

Vermiculture vs Composting:

- Worms create a compost material that is far superior than any compost that is produced without their assistance
- The compost material that is created by worms is smaller than 2 microns
- Vermicompost added to soil creates a material that has better water retention, aeration, drainage and stability
- Vermicompost contains more antibiotic properties against pathogens than regular compost and higher amounts of natural plant growth hormones
- Worms have the ability to reduce all bacteria that is pathogenic to animals and people

Composting worms have only three jobs: <u>eat</u>, poop, and make babies. Your job is to manage the worms in a way to maximize all three.

The keyhole garden approach is based on composting organic materials right inside of their ultimate destination, thus eliminating a very time consuming and labor intensive step in traditional gardening approaches.

15 Uses for Vinegar In Your Gardens

Keep Fruit Flies Away

Protect your fruits and fruit trees by making a fruit fly deterrent or rather attractant that they get stuck in. To make: use 1 cup of water, 1/2 cup of apple cider vinegar, 1/4 cup of sugar and 1 tbsp of molasses. Mix it all together. Using empty and clean tin cans, make a wire or sturdy string hanger and hang in your fruit trees. This will attract the flies and they will get stuck. A similar concoction can be made to trap fruit flies in the house too!

Help Acid Loving Plants

By using vinegar in the water, you can increase the iron in the soil, which acid loving plants like! To do this for hard water areas, add 1 cup of vinegar to 1 gallon of tap water for watering your acid loving plants.

Keep Ants Away

Spray your ant infested areas and ant hills with undiluted vinegar and this will solve your ant problem! You may need to reapply a few times for a few days.

Deter Rabbits, Raccoons and Cats

These animals hate the smell of vinegar and it will keep them out of your garden naturally and safely. It is best to soak something in full strength vinegar for an hour or so and then place around your garden. Corn cobs, cotton balls, rags, etc.

Rust Eliminator

If you have any rusty garden tools, yard tools or yard pieces, you can remove the rust by either soaking or spraying undiluted vinegar and rinse/wipe clean.

Kill Mold in Containers

It is important to start with clean pots or seedling starter containers so that you can reduce your chances of mold or fungus on your plants. Vinegar and water together can act as a natural mold killer in your containers before replanting.

Reduce Brown Spots in Your Yard

This one sounds weird and it will only work if you have a dog. Every time you fill your dog's water bowl, add a tablespoon of vinegar to the bowl. It is harmless for the dog, but as your dog pees in your yard, it will cure the brown spots..... Now if only you can train him/her to pee in the right places! ☺

Kill Grass and Weeds in Unwanted Areas

Spraying or pouring straight vinegar on your weeds or grass that has overgrown onto driveways or cement will kill them and stop them from growing for a time. Also, adding salt to the mixture may be a little more effective in this process. You also may need to do this a few times, but it is safer and a natural alternative.

Keep Your Garden Flowers Longer

If you want to enjoy fruits of your labors indoors with your cut flowers, you can make them last a little longer by making your own feed for your flowers. Just add 2 tablespoons vinegar and 2 tablespoons sugar in a 1-quart vase of water to your flowers. Trim the stems of the flowers and change this solution about every 5 days or as needed.

Potted Plant Fertilizer

Fertilizer your potted plants and purify the water by adding 2 tablespoons of apple cider vinegar to 1 gallon of water before you water your potted plants.

Feed Plants

Give your plants extra nutrients with a solution of vinegar, sugar and water. First, mix 1 tablespoon of vinegar and 1 tablespoon of sugar for every 8 ounces of water. Then feed your plants as needed!

Clean Garden Tools

Easily clean your garden tools naturally with a bucket of vinegar and water. Just pour a few ounces of vinegar in a gallon of water and soak and rinse your tools before putting away or storing! You can also mix 3 ounces of vinegar in 32 oz bottle and spray it on to clean! This will also naturally kill fungus that may develop on your tools from the soil.

Kill Slugs

Just use undiluted vinegar sprayed directly on to kill slugs and snails that eat your lettuce and veggies.

Plant Fungicide

Similar to the <u>damping off issue on your seedlings</u>, you can take a mixture of 2 tablespoons of vinegar and brewed chamomile tea to spray on your plants outdoors to kill fungus and mold that may have grown.

Pecking Chickens

If you have backyard chickens, they can get to a point where they start pecking at each other. You can help solve this problem naturally! How? Just add a tablespoon of cider vinegar to their drinking water and they will stop pecking at each other! It is a safe and natural solution!

<u>Mosquito Spray:</u>

Two or more full bulbs of garlic smashed flat with your coffee mug; peel and put into a screw top gallon jug. Add 1/2 cup of minced garlic, then fill with water. Keep at room temp. for two days. You use a 2 1/2 gallon sprayer; with 2 cups of the juice strained through a cloth, 1 cup of vegetable oil, and 3 tbls. of liquid soap; then fill with water to the line. Shake well, pump; then spray wherever you want. This will kill them dead and work at least till the rain comes. The soap helps it stick to their wings and other surfaces. Keep adding water and minced garlic to the jug to keep it filled and smelly.

Mosquito spray II:

Use 1/2 cup pine cleaner, 2tbls of liquid soap in a quart garden spray bottle; then fill with water. Shake and spray. The only thing that it won't kill in 30 seconds is hard shell beetles.

Natural Fire Ant Control:

Use ground cinnamon powder to kill fire ants. Sprinkle the whole mound with cinnamon.

Ingredients:

- 1/2 liter of alcohol (this is approximately 17 oz)
- 100 gram of whole cloves or approximately 3.5oz
- 100 ml of baby oil or similar (almond, sesame, chamomile, lavender, fennel etc) 3.4 oz

Preparation:

Leave cloves to marinate in alcohol four days. Stir every morning and evening and after 4 days add the oil. It is now ready to use.

How to use:

Gently rub a few drops into the skin of the arms and legs. Observe the mosquitoes fleeing the room. This is excellent to repel fleas on pets too.

Alcohol Sprays
The idea of using rubbing alcohol as a spray for plants pests has been around for years. It can cause leaf damage on African Violets, and Apple trees.
Protection offered: Alcohol sprays work on aphids, mealy bugs, scale insects, thrips and whiteflies. Alcohol sprays have been used successfully on houseplants and tropical foliage plants. Most of these have heavy, waxy cuticles that are not easily burned.
How to Make: Use only 70% isopropyl alcohol (rubbing alcohol): mix 1 to 2 cups alcohol per quart of water. Using undiluted alcohol as a spray is very risky for plants. You can also mix up an insecticidal soap spray according to the dilution on the label but substitute alcohol for half of the water required.
How to Use: Since alcohol can damage plants always test your spray mix on a few leaves or plants first. Tests results should show up within 2 or 3 days.

Tomato Leaf Nightshade family plants, such as tomatoes, potatoes and tobacco, have toxic compounds called alkaloids in their leaves. These toxins are water soluble and can be soaked from chopped leaves and made into home-made sprays. These sprays also work by attracting natural pest enemies. The good bugs follow the smell of the spray in looking for prey.
Protection Offered: Tomato leaf sprays have been used to protect plants from aphids. Also, spraying tomato leaf

spray on corn may reduce corn earworm damage. The corn earworm is also called the tomato fruit worm, as it also attacks tomato plants. A scientific study has shown that corn plants sprayed with tomato leaf spray attracted significantly more Trichogramma wasps to parasitize the corn earworm eggs than the unsprayed did.

How to Make: Soak 1 to 2 cups of chopped or mashed tomato leaves in 2 cups of water overnight. Strain through cheesecloth or fine mesh. Add about 2 more cups of water to the strained liquid, and spray. For aphid control, be sure to thoroughly cover the leaf undersides, especially of lower leaves and growing tips of plants where aphids congregate.

How to Use: Spray plants thoroughly, particularly undersides of lower leaves and growing tips where aphids congregate. While this spray is not poisonous to humans on contact, use care in handling, especially if you are allergic to the nightshade family.

Garlic Oil Sprays:

Organic gardeners have long been familiar with the repellent or toxic affect of garlic oil on pests. When it is combined with mineral oil and pure soap, as it is in the recipe that follows, devised at the Henry Doubleday Research Association in England, it becomes an effective insecticide. Some studies also suggest that a garlic oil spray has fungicidal properties.

Protection Offered: Good results, with quick kill, have been noted against aphids, cabbage loopers, earwigs, June bugs, leafhoppers, squash bugs and whiteflies. The spray does not appear to harm adult lady beetles, and some gardeners have found that it doesn't work against the Colorado potato beetles, grape leaf skeletonizers, grasshoppers, red ants, or sow bugs.

How to Make: Soak 3 ounces of finely minced garlic

cloves in 2 teaspoons of mineral oil for at least 24 hours. Slowly add 1 pint of water that has 1/4 ounce liquid soap or commercial insecticide soap mixed into it. Stir thoroughly and strain into a glass jar for storage. Use at a rate of 1 to 2 Tablespoons of mixture to a pint of water. If this is effective, try a more dilute solution in order to use as little as possible.
How to Use: Spray plants carefully to ensure thorough coverage. To check for possible leaf damage to sensitive ornamentals from the oil and soap in the spray, do a test spray on a few leaves or plants first. If no leaf damage occurs in 2 or 3 days, go ahead and spray more.

Herbal Sprays

Many organic farmers are familiar with using sprays made from aromatic herbs to repel pests from the garden plants. Several recent studies confirm the repellent effect of such sprays. The <u>essential oil</u> of Sage and Thyme and the alcohol extracts such as Hyssop, Rosemary, Sage, Thyme, and White Clover can be used in this manner. They have been shown to reduce the number of eggs laid and the amount of feeding damage to cabbage by caterpillars of Diamond back moths and large white butterflies. Sprays made from Tansy have demonstrated a repellent effect on imported cabbageworm on cabbage, reducing the number of eggs laid on the plants. Teas made from Wormwood or Nasturtiums are reputed to repel aphids from fruit trees, and sprays made from ground or blended Catnip, Chives, Feverfew, Marigolds, or Rue have also been used by gardeners against pests that feed on leaves.
Protection Offered: Try herbal sprays against any leaf-eating pests and make note of what works for future reference.
How to Make: In General, herbal sprays are made by mashing or blending 1 to 2 cups of fresh leaves with 2 to 4

cups of water and leaving them to soak overnight. Or you can make herbal tea by pouring the same amount of boiling water over 2 to 4 cups fresh or 1 to 2 cups dry leaves and leaving them to steep until cool. Strain the water through a cheese cloth before spraying and dilute further with 2 to 4 cups water. Add a very small amount of non-detergent liquid soap (1/4 teaspoon in 1 to 2 quarts of water) to help spray stick to leaves and spread better. You can also buy commercial <u>essential herbal oils</u> and dilute with water to make a spray. Experiment with proportions, starting with a few drops of oil per cup of water.

How to Use: Spray plants thoroughly, especially undersides of leaves, and repeat at weekly intervals if necessary.

"Hot" Dusts

Black pepper, chili pepper, dill, ginger, paprika, and red pepper all contain capsaicin, a compound shown to repel insects. Synthetic capsaicin is also available for field use. Researchers have found that as little as 1/25 ounce of capsaicin sprinkled around an onion plant reduced the number of onion maggot eggs laid around the plant by 75%, compared to a control plant.

Protection Offered: Capsaicin-containing dusts repel onion maggots from seedlings, as well as other root maggot flies from cabbage family plants and carrots. Pepper dusts around the base of the plants help repel ants, which is desirable in a garden where ants often protect and maintain aphid colonies on plants.

How to Make: It can be rather expensive to buy enough packaged pepper dusts to sprinkle throughout your garden. However, if you grow and dry your own red peppers, chili peppers, or dill, you can make lots of dust at low cost. Use a mortar and pestle to grind the peppers, or

dill, including the seeds, to dust. Be careful handling the hot peppers because they irritate sensitive skin.
How to Use: Sprinkle along seeded rows of onions, cabbage, or carrots, in a band at least 6 inches wider than the row or planting bed. A fine sprinkling will suffice, but the more dust you use, the better the effect. Renew after a heavy rain or irrigation. To protect plants from ants, sprinkle around the base of plants in an area as wide as the widest leaves.

Pyrethrum

The dried, powdered flowers of the pyrethrum daisy, Tanacetum cinerarifolium, were used as early as 1880 to control mosquitoes. The popularity of pyrethrum insecticides waned when synthetic insecticides were introduced, but they are now enjoying a commercial comeback. Many new products formulated with natural pyrethrums are available. Pyrethrums are the insecticidal chemicals extracted from the pyrethrum daisy.

Do not confuse them with pyrethroids, the term for a new class of synthetic pesticides. Pyrethrums, which are mainly concentrated in the seeds of the flower head, are a contact insecticide, meaning the insect only has to touch the substance to be affected. Pyrethrums have a quick knockdown effect on insects: Flying insects are paralyzed. Pyrethrums can be applied up to one day before harvest because they are quickly destroyed by light and heat and are not persistent in the environment. Pyrethrums will kill lady beets but do not appear to be harmful to bees. They are toxic to fish and to the aquatic insects and other small animals that fish eat. Pyrethrums do not seem to be toxic to birds or mammals.

Protection Offered: Pyrethrums are registered for flowers, fruits, and vegetables, including greenhouse crops. They are effective on many chewing and sucking insects, including most aphids, cabbage loopers, celery leaftiers, codling moth, Colorado potato beetles, leafhoppers, Mexican bean beetles, spider mites, and stink bugs, several species of thrips, tomato pinworms, and whiteflies. They are especially good against flies, gnats, mosquitoes, and stored products pests. Flea beetles are not affected, nor are imported cabbageworms, diamondback moths, pear psylla, and tarnished plant bugs.

How to Make: If you grow your own pyrethrum daisies, you'll have the main ingredient for a make-it-yourself spray. The concentration of pyrethrums is at its peak when the flowers are in full bloom, from the time the first row of florets open on the central disk opens to the time all the florets are open. Pick flowers in full bloom and hang them in a sheltered, dark spot to dry. Once the flowers have dried thoroughly, grind them to a fine powder, using a mortar and pestle, old blender or small hammer mill. Mix with water and add a few drops of liquid soap. Store in a glass jar and keep the lid tightly closed, because the mixture looses activity if left open.

You'll have to experiment with the amount of water to add, because the concentration of pyre thins in the flowers is an unknown variable. If the spray you make does not seem to kill insects, use less water the next time you make the concentrated spray. Also keep in mind whole flower heads stay potent longer so do not grind until ready to use.

How to Use: Pyrethrums are more effective at lower temperatures, so for best results, apply in early evening when temperatures are lower. Spray both the upper and lower surfaces of the leaves, because spray must directly contact the insects such as thrips that hide in leaf sheaths and crevices. The first spray will excite them and bring them out of hiding, the second will kill them. Never use pyrethrum products around waterways and ponds.

Nicotine

One of the top three insecticides in the 1880s, nicotine in several forms is still widely used. Nicotine comes from the tobacco plant and is extremely toxic to insects. The great advantage of home-made nicotine tea is that it is very short lived, retaining its toxicity for only a few hours after spraying. It is relatively nonhazardous to bees and lady beetles because of its short persistence.

Protection Offered: Nicotine is effective against ground and soil pests, especially root aphids and fungus gnats, and on many leaf-chewing insects, such as aphids, immature scales, leafhoppers, thrips, leafminers, pear psylla, and asparagus beetle larvae.

How to Make: You can brew your own batch of nicotine tea by soaking tobacco leaves or cigarette butts in water to make a spray. Soak 1 cup of dried, crushed tobacco leaves, or an equivalent amount of cigarette butts, in one gallon of warm water with 1/4 teaspoon pure soap added. Strain the mixture through cheesecloth after it has soaked for 1/2 hour. The solution will keep for several weeks if stored in a tightly closed container.

How to Use: For soil pests, pour the spray mixture onto the soil in the area of the stem base and root zone. For leaf pests, spray leaves thoroughly, especially the undersides.

Nicotine can be absorbed by plant leaves and remain there for several weeks. to be safe, use nicotine only on young plants and only up to one month before harvest. It's probably safest not to spray nicotine on eggplant, peppers or tomatoes. While most tobacco cultivars now grown are resistant to tobacco mosaic virus, nicotine sprays could contain the pathogen, which will infect nightshade family crops.

Contender Beans

9

PASSIONATE ABOUT PERMACULTURE

Goji Berries

Growing Goji berries (also known as wolfberries) is a great option for introducing the "superfood" fruits into your garden. Now most would not call this plant as one to be thought of bugging out with it as a candidate. The Chinese railroad workers brought it with them as a primary cooking and fresh consumption mainstay and planted it all over the west everywhere the tracks led. I planted mine in places of honor in my keyhole gardens from KeyholeFarm.com as a permanent integral part of my garden.

If I ever had to bug out from Prepper Shack you can be assured the plants are going with me in some form or fashion. I have other Goji plantings on the property but these are new cuttings from a mother plant I bought off Ebay. Even though they are young I will still get berries this year. Goji Berry soup for health benefits and a better nutritional diet is part of my new regime of being ready to be my own health care provider no matter what.

I really like my keyhole garden system, vermiculture assures that I get maximum nutritional benefits from my crops as well being able to control the beds environment more closely. As an added benefit I also think of them as defensive barriers or an apocalyptic fighting

position if one considers such necessary, because that much dirt can easily stop most any bullet fired into it.

The Lycium barbarum variety of Goji Berry Plants are a perennial in zones 3 to 10, they are actually quite remarkably heat and cold tolerant. Goji plants are also deciduous, which just means that they drop their leaves every year, usually once the first frost hits.

- **Protein:** Goji berries are one of the very few plant-based foods that can provide you with a complete protein. This means that the berries contain all of the amino acids, which are the building blocks of proteins that your body cannot make for itself. Meats and dairy products contain all of these essential amino acids, but most plants do not. Vegetarians and vegans typically combine foods like beans and grains to get a complete protein, but Goji berries can give you all of them in one package
- The Goji plant begins flowering in the second year with maximum fruit production in the 4th or 5th year.
- Goji (*Lycium barbarum*), a native of the Himalayan valleys of Tibet, has come to be known as wolfberry to some in the West and these berries aren't for everyone either — anyone who uses blood thinners or takes diabetic medication may have a negative reaction eating Goji berries, according to WebMD.

When in doubt, ask your doctor first. Goji berries can interfere with blood thinners like warfarin. If you take this medication, you should not eat the berries.

☐ Approximate **yield per plant:** Up to 6.7 pounds (3 kg) depending on climate
☐ Life **of plant:** Up to 90 years

☐ Companion **plants:**

- Companions: n/a
- Avoid: Avoid planting near potatoes and tomatoes

Vitamin E (very rarely found in fruits, usually only found in grains, seeds, and nuts.)

More protein than whole wheat (13% more), the Goji Berry displays an insulin-like action that is effective in fat decomposition.

Antioxidant-rich - According to Jodi Helmer, the author of *Goji Berries: Antioxidant Supreme*, goji berries are an excellent source of antioxidants such as polyphenols, flavonoids, carotenoids and vitamins A, C and E. In fact, the Goji berry contains approximately 500 times more vitamin C per weight than an orange and considerably more beta-carotene than carrots. These findings are reinforced by the Goji berries' high Oxygen Radical Absorbance Capacity (ORAC) score of 3,290, which shows that they contain much larger concentrations of antioxidants than most other fruits. Since antioxidants help neutralize the cell-damaging effects of free radicals, eating more antioxidant-rich foods like Goji berries can help guard us from degenerative diseases such as rheumatoid arthritis, Alzheimer's disease and most types of cancer.

High in nutrients - Though Goji berries are best-known for their antioxidant activity, they also contain an impressive number of vitamins and minerals. According to Paul Gross in his report, *The Top 20 Superfruits*, a quarter cup of Goji berries contains 11 essential vitamins and 22 trace minerals, including 24 percent of our RDI of potassium, 18 percent of our RDI of zinc and a whopping 100 percent of our RDI of iron, copper and riboflavin. They also contain 8 polysaccharides, a primary source of dietary fiber.

Fortify Liver
Goji berries contain a group of neutral chemical compounds called betaines which are the secret behind its long history of use to support liver health. Betaines have been shown to reduce fatty deposits in the liver which may result from any number of lifestyle factors (alcohol use, diabetes, diet, etc.) While controlled studies involving laboratory rats far outnumber those performed on humans, the history of the Goji berry speaks for itself.

Protection From UV Radiation

The juice derived from Goji berries can reduce the amount of damage done by ultraviolet radiation. According to a study published in January 2010 in "Photochemical and Photobiological Sciences," mice that consumed Goji berry juice had a significantly reduced inflammatory sunburn response to prolonged simulated ultraviolet radiation. Researchers believe that some of the antioxidants found in Goji berries are responsible for this protection, preventing the oxidative damage that would otherwise induce the inflammatory response. So consuming these while working in the garden under that hot sun just makes good sense.

Protection of Eye Health

While it is very difficult if not impossible to "fix" your eyes if you already have poor vision (short of having surgery), it is possible to protect your eyes from further damage using natural remedies. According to a study published in February 2011 in "Optometry and Vision Science," daily supplementation of Goji berries over the course of 90 days significantly aids in the prevention of soft drusen accumulation in the eyes of elderly patients, an early warning sign of age-related macular degeneration. This exact mechanism behind this effect is currently unclear. Taurine, a compound found in Goji berries, is also beneficial in slowing the development of eye conditions related to diabetes.

Goji berries contain two key nutrients that support vision: lutein and zeaxanthin. Studies show that consuming high amounts of lutein and zeaxanthin lowers the risk for developing age-related macular degeneration, cataracts, and other eye diseases. So, what all this means, is that you are growing your own cheaper and better form of eye vitamins!

Prevent vision loss - Goji berries contain high concentrations of the carotenoid zeaxanthin which has been recognized for its ability to protect eyes from damage caused by oxidation and for reducing the risk of age-related macular degeneration (AMD) which is the number one cause of blindness in human beings over the age of 65. Hopefully, we all plan on making it to age 65 and knowing the risks that are indicated in this study, doesn't it make good sense to be including this in our diet now instead of finding out we should have been doing it later?

Studies have also been performed regarding the polysaccharides in Goji berries and how they may reduce or prevent damage to the retina and optic nerve.

According to a study published in the 2005 issue of the *British Journal of Nutrition*, Goji berries contain properties that prevent the risk of vision loss. Researchers at *Hong Kong Polytechnic University* fed 14 healthy volunteers a serving of 15 grams of Goji berries daily for 28 days while comparing their blood levels to 13 control volunteers. After 28 days, the volunteers who consumed the fruits experienced significantly raised zeaxanthin levels in the blood (zeaxanthin is an antioxidant present in Goji berries that helps preserve eyesight). Therefore, if you're suffering from poor or deteriorating eyesight, consider adding more Goji berries to your diet.

Blood-glucose Regulation

Goji berries are one of a handful of fruits that can be safely enjoyed by diabetics. With a GI value of only 29 (less than 40 is considered low) Goji berries won't cause a spike in blood-glucose levels like some fruits. There have also been studies which show that Goji berries may have a positive impact on reducing insulin resistance. Regular ingestion of Goji berries can also promote healthy weight, triglyceride, and cholesterol levels.

Heart disease: Consuming Goji berries has been shown to increase the amount of an enzyme in the human body called superoxide dismutase. This is the enzyme that prevents cholesterol from oxidizing. In its oxidized form, cholesterol is harmful to your heart and contributes to heart disease. By eating more Goji berries you can lower your risk of dangerous heart conditions.

Defend Your Brain Preppers

Possibly due to its high levels of calcium and B vitamins, Goji berries have also been shown to protect the mind against degenerative disorders like Alzheimer's disease. In fact, its ability to defend the nervous system is one of the few health benefits of this amazing "superfruit" that has been scientifically researched and confirmed to be effective on humans. So if you're having trouble with memory, mental clarity, or any other neurological functions, you just might benefit from a handful of dried Goji berries mixed in with your morning cereal or smoothie. You might also ask yourself in a starvation on the horizon environment of living longterm in a bug out situation that you may expect such mental afflictions and be planning accordingly. Do you see why I list Goji Berries in this book now?

Anti-Aging

Longevity and anti-aging properties: The fruits of the Goji plant have long been associated in China with longevity. Modern research has found that certain oils in the berries, called sesquiterpinoids can increase your production of human growth hormone. No other plant has been shown to have such an effect on these hormones. As you age, your production of this hormone decreases. By consuming the berries, you can up the production and may see the anti-aging effects in your appearance and overall health. Goji berries are full of antioxidants that help to protect DNA from damage caused by free-radicals – the biological waste byproducts that our bodies naturally produce simply by living. Goji berries also contain useful amino acids and minerals that aid our bodies in the process of repairing and regenerating cells. What this means is that a daily serving of Goji berries or Goji juice can actually help to slow or in some cases even reverse the signs of aging.

Fortify Immune System

Goji berries have traditionally been used to fortify the immune system against infection and recent studies have given us probable cause to believe it works. Carotenoid beta-carotene and amino-acid Cystine found in Goji berries are both recognized for their positive impact on immune function. Goji berries also contain zinc which is crucial for immune health and one of the most widely-used remedies for the prevention of otherwise incurable viral illnesses such as the common cold. Furthermore, the polysaccharides contained in Goji berries have been shown to stimulate increased immune function.

Cancer-Fighting Properties

Small, fleshy berries like the Goji berry contain antioxidant compounds known as polyphenols that could protect against the development of cancer. These antioxidants fight against, diminish and repair cell damage that results from inflammation and oxidative stress from free radicals, preventing the likelihood of cancerous tumor development. Antioxidants like those in Goji berries may also improve the effectiveness of chemotherapy by weakening tumor cells, reports a study published in 2008 in the "Journal of Agricultural and Food Chemistry."

Benefits of Goji (cancer)

The chemical component that gives Goji this positive effect is beta-sitosterol (also called cinchol. This compound is found in the bright red berries themselves and beta-sitosterol can affectively decrease the size of overgrown cells; In fact it can even induce apoptosis (cell suicide) of tumor cells. Apoptosis is a process during which the body induces cell suicide for dysfunctional or abnormal cells which can potentially cause harm to the body if their replication continues.

This property of Goji berries makes it a more commonly used treatment for prostate enlargement. After men reach their 40s, the cells of the prostate gland enlarge to a certain extent. When it persists it can develop into a condition called benign prostatic hyperplasia (BPH). If left unaddressed the enlargement of this gland can cause obstruction of the urinary tract thus making urination difficult and, in some instances, painful for older men. In the case of prostate cancer, these cells enlarge and divide out of control causing them to damage normal cells tissues surrounding these abnormal cells. And this can do extensive damage to normal body functioning. Because the beta-sitosterol in Goji effectively reduces the size of these swollen cells without serious side affects it is becoming used commonly by physicians. It is used as a precautionary treatment but in patients with cancers, it can be used along with other medications to assist in the reduction of tumor cells (no known drug interactions have been documented for beta-sitosterol).

Improved Feelings of Well-being

If vitality is your aim, this is your berry. According to a study published in May 2008 in the "Journal of Alternative and Complementary Medicine," drinking juice derived from Goji berries has a positive effect on overall well-being. In a SHTF situation or for that matter in everyday life I think we can all benefit as well as know others that need this plant in their diets. Study participants drank Goji berry juice daily for a period of 15 days, reporting perceived levels of energy, quality of sleep and feelings of happiness. After 15 days, both the Goji berry group and the placebo group reported higher levels of happiness, but the Goji berry group also reported improved energy levels, lower fatigue, and lower stress and improved digestive function. While these measures are subjective, the findings are statistically significant for mine as well as your consideration and further research in dealing with disaster related Post Traumatic stress (PTSD) syndrome. Because they contain such a wide variety of vitamins, minerals, amino-acids, and oils that have a positive impact on hormone production and overall health of the human body, it's no wonder that science has proven that Goji berries just make you feel good. In a post apocalyptic world or when a tornado just took your barn down, you want to feel better and get over it right without relying on alcohol or other substances to numb the blow right?

Improve male fertility - Goji berries have long been considered a male aphrodisiac in China, and more studies are starting to confirm these allegations. According to a Chinese study published in the July 2006 issue of *Life Sciences*, for example, rats that were fed Goji berries maintained testicular function when subjected to heat. The researchers also found that certain constituents in Goji berries regulated the release of sexual hormones, boosted hormone levels and improved the quality and quantity of sperm in male rats. Ok, all you lab rats living after a major disaster, are we going to repopulate the world or just get happy trying?

How to Grow Goji Berry Plants

Once established, Goji berries are incredibly easy to grow. They'll grow in almost any type of soil, and can even thrive in poor soil, as they are used to the mountainous regions in the Himalayas. They are reasonably drought-tolerant, and will even grow in partial shade (though you'll get more berries from them if you grow them in full sun). Once established Goji berry plants are easy to grow and maintain. They can grow in almost any soil type, light-sandy, medium-loamy, heavy-clay or any combination of the three. Even soils of poor soil structure and nutrient content will grow

Goji plants, but soils of better quality will allow for better flowering and fruiting characteristics. Are you all following me with the bug in bug out aspect of having a highly documented beneficial plant that you have access now to replacing that pharmaceutical crap that will not be available come grid down or healthcare insurance loss? A well drained soil is a must as Goji berry plants will not grow well in wet or soggy conditions. Goji plants have an aggressive root system and are quite drought tolerant after they are established.

Goji Berry plants are very adaptable, but for the very best results, test your soil, and then adjust the pH to between 6.8 – 8.1 if you are able. You can add lime to raise the pH if necessary or aluminum sulfate to lower it, other instructions for sweetening your soil or adding acid is included in this book.

Flowers
The Goji berry grows into a large shrub reaching heights of 7-10 feet with vines that can reach 10 feet. After two years the bushes will start to fruit, and from four years you'll start to get very heavy yields. In early summer the bushes will produce small, delicate, trumpet-shaped flowers that will be either white or purple. Both colored flowers can feature on one plant, so they provide visual interest before the berry production begins.

The berries will begin to set in autumn. The ripe fruit are sweet and juicy and almost shiny in appearance. The flowers will continue to bloom right up until the first frosts, however, so your plants will be red, white and purple throughout late summer and autumn.

They are beautiful to have in your garden, delicious, nutritious, and cheap and easy to grow. If you want health-boosting berries on tap you should consider investing in a Goji berry bush or two.

GROW GOJI BERRY PLANTS IN CONTAINERS

Goji Berry plants can easily be grown in containers on your deck or patio. Goji plant roots like to grow deep, but the plant itself will stop growing once the roots touch the bottom of the container, so they won't grow as large as the plants grow in the ground. One advantage is that you may very well see Goji berries in the first or second season, rather than the third, which is normally the case when they are grown in the ground.

So you've received your bare root plants. They will survive for awhile without being planted, but we recommend that you plant them as soon as possible. We also suggest that you get them established inside, in a sunny location, before moving them outside, also to a sunny location. Your Goji plant will appreciate some afternoon shade if you live in a very hot climate (Temps above 100°F).

- Place the bare root plants in a jar or container with room-temperature water and allow them to soak for about 15-minutes.
- Prepare your container. We recommend a container at least as deep as a five-gallon bucket, but it does not have to be wide. Your container or pot should have drainage holes in the bottom (if it doesn't—make some), so you may also want to provide a drain pan for the container to sit in.
- Mix about 1/3 sand to 2/3 soil in order to provide the best growing medium and drainage, though any good potting soil will work. In hot, dry areas, we recommend Premier Pro-Mix Ultimate Container Mix. Fill the container, leaving 2 to 3-inches at the top.
- Dig a hole in the middle of the container a couple of inches deeper than to the crown of the plant (where the roots meet the stem), pushing loose soil back in until with the roots lightly resting on the soil in the hole, the crown is level with the top of the soil.
- Push the soil back in, filling around the roots and up to the crown, gently tamping as you go.

- Water well and push more soil around the plant if necessary, watering again to let the soil settle.
- You should continue to keep your Goji plant moist, but not overly wet, until you see new growth sprouting, usually in about 2-weeks.
- Apply an inch or two of mulch in order to help with moisture retention (and because it looks nice). If you mulch, you will depend upon touch to check soil moisture, or water into a large reservoir under the planter so it is wicked from the bottom up.

You may see flowers, after which fruit will follow, the first season, depending upon when you plant; but more than likely it will be the second season. Remember that containerized plants will feel the heat and cold more because their roots are in soil above the ground. Be weather-aware, providing adequate moisture when it is extremely hot and dry, as containerized plants will usually dry out quicker and in order to provide protection for your plant if the temperatures become really cold.

GROW GOJI BERRY PLANTS IN THE GROUND

You can grow Goji Berry plants in the ground in any relatively sunny location, as long as you have room for expansion. Adult Goji plants can grow up to 8-feet high and wide, though some gardeners prune their Goji plants to keep them within a desired size range. You can even grow Goji bushes as a hedge or you can train them to a trellis, in which case, they can get as tall as 10-feet.

To make this really simple and to give your Goji Berry Plant the best start, we recommend that you start it in a container, though you don't need a 5-gallon size. In fact, you can buy a 4 to 6-inch peat pot and not even have to worry about taking it back out of the pot to transplant it. This will greatly reduce the stress involved with transplanting; further ensuring your Goji plant will thrive. If you are starting it in a container, you just follow steps 1 through 7 above, at which point you can transplant your Goji plant into the ground. Goji plants growing in the ground will sometimes start to produce fruit the second season, but will not go into full production until the third year.

If you are putting it directly into the ground:

- Choose a sunny site if you live anywhere *but* in the desert southwest, where you will either want to have shade or be able to put up a shade cloth during the hottest part of the day.
- Follow step 1 above, and then prepare your soil, testing and amending it if needed.
- Skip to step 4, and continue through step 8 above, applying mulch immediately, rather than waiting, and carefully monitoring soil moisture. It is critical that it not be allowed

to dry out until you see new growth start to sprout, usually in about two weeks.

How many plants should I plant?

A 30 foot row with 15 plants has the potential to produce up to 100 pounds of berries per year, which would supply about 80% of a person's annual nutrient needs. Three ounces of dried berries have approximately 80% of a person's daily nutrient requirements (not calories). So you're not going to be living off the Goji but you will not be worrying about your loss of access to vitamin supplements grid down or economically challenged.

PRUNING YOUR GOJI BERRY PLANTS

Pruning is normally done in the winter, but they can also be gently trimmed throughout the season to shape the canopy and to improve berry yield.

You will not want to prune them heavily the first year. Identify the largest, healthy shoot, which will be the main trunk. Gradually remove the lower lateral shoots, with the goal in mind of keeping the trunk clear for the first 15-inches, and then when your Goji plant reaches 24-inches , remove the growing tip in order to stimulate the growth of additional side branches.

Your Goji will grow and thrive, even if you never prune it once. However, it will be easier to harvest with some selective pruning. Simply shorten the horizontal branches by about half to two-thirds in early spring, just as the buds begin to break. Plants can withstand severe pruning, but fruiting may be minimal in the following season. To prune adult plants, you just remove the branches above the height that you wish to keep. You should maintain clearance from the ground up to about 15-inches. You can also identify any ineffective branches. These usually grow very fast, straight and smooth and will not be very productive, so if they aren't essential to the overall look, they can simply be removed. Remember that Goji Berry plants grow similar to a weeping willow. If allowed to grow un-pruned you can end up with a mighty ugly plant, though "ugly" is only in the eye of the beholder, and you may thoroughly enjoy this natural look. You should always prune the plant after a heavy berry season as berries are produced on new growth only.

Drying Goji berries is a great way to store berries that aren't eaten fresh. You can add these to cereals or salads and make them into tea.

To dry them...

1. Spread your Goji berries on a baking sheet making sure they are not touching

2. Set the oven to its lowest temperature and leave the door slightly open
3. Bake the berries for up to 12 hours until they have dried
4. Allow them to cool
5. Store in an airtight jar

Berries stored in this way can last up to a year.

☐ **Storage life (dried):** up to one year if dried but NOT refrigerated

☐ **Storage life (dried and refrigerated):** up to two years if dried and refrigerated

PESTS- Other than attracting birds and other animals, Goji berries are very pest- and disease-resistant. This makes them a very low maintenance plant. As mentioned previously, do not plant them near potatoes or tomatoes as this may result in blight-type diseases.

Artichoke: These thistle relatives, properly called globe artichokes, aren't the most soft and cuddly vegetables, but yield a large tasty flower bud. Growing artichokes does take a bit of room in the garden, as they can grow to 6 feet or more in height, and like most perennial vegetables, a couple of years of growth is often necessary before they've matured to the point that you can harvest enough flowers to grace your table. While they can be started from seed, artichokes can also be planted from dividing an established patch, or from starter plants that may be available from the garden center.

Collards: Most people don't get too excited when they hear that collard greens are for dinner, but few people know that these greens have been ranked as one of the most nutritionally dense foods in existence. In the ANDI score rating, which stand for aggregate nutritional density index, collard greens have been given a score of 1000 out of 1000. The leaves of this plant are literally packed with energy of Mother Nature. They contain more protein by weight than beef.

Tree collards another species usually found in California but gaining in popularity everywhere are also an excellent source of vitamins K, A, C, folate, manganese and calcium. Their high concentration of fiber means they'll keep you regular too. Tree collards can be eaten any way that regular collard greens can be eaten, as a wrap for a raw burrito, sautéed with other vegetables, or as a raw green juice.

To grow tree collards, you'll need to get a plant from a friend or nursery. There are two varieties available, white veined and purple veined. (Either is great.)

Chaya:

Grow this miracle spinach in every home and add it to your regular diet. All you need to know about it is that the plant needs cooking before you eat it. This plant isn't scary – it just needs cooking before you can eat it. Big deal.

Chaya, the Tree Spinach or Mayan miracle plant *Cnidoscolus chayamansa*

Flowers are very fragrant with a nice spicy scent!

Height: 6-8 ft.

Flowers: Blooms repeatedly, Bloom Color: White/Near White. This plant is attractive to bees, butterflies and/or birds.

Foliage: Grown for Foliage, Evergreen, Shiny/Glossy-Textured, Succulent.

CULTURE: Full Sun to Partial Shade.

Taste The flavor is actually very mild, less bitter than spinach, and also less acidic. These plants provide a cheap and easily produced source of highly nutritious greens.

Chaya is a perennial leaf vegetable. This is a must-grow vegetable for anyone in USDA Zone 8 and south. Further north it's probably still worth growing – I'd just keep it in a pot through the worst of the winter.

Here is a contribution of the unforgettable Maya Indians, whom we have abandoned," is the wistful introduction to a pamphlet on the *Chaya* plant, from Desarollo Integral de la Familia (DIF), which goes on to call *Chaya* "an ideal food and medicine." The ancient Mayan's used Chaya as a dietary staple for centuries because of its amazing nutritional qualities which gave people the strength they needed for their often harsh work and physically demanding lives.

They also recognized Chaya as having many medicinal qualities to keep the mind and body strong and healthy. Despite the superfood qualities of bountiful plant, the use of Chaya has become largely forgotten. Chaya plants are extremely hearty, they can grow in poor soils and have also shown to survive in freezing temperatures, quickly sprouting back up when it warms up.

According to the National Institute of Nutrition in Mexico City, ingesting Chaya will:

- Improve blood circulation,
- help digestion,
- improve vision,
- disinflame veins and hemorrhoids,
- help lower cholesterol,
- help reduce weight,
- prevent coughs,
- augment calcium in the bones,
- decongest and disinfect the lungs,

- prevent anemia by replacing iron in the blood,
- improve memory and brain function and
- combat arthritis and diabetes.

Chaya is a large, leafy shrub reaching a height of about 6 to 8 feet. Chaya was introduced into Cuba, and from there into Florida. In South Florida it is often found as a rank shrub, but seldom is appreciated for its food value as a vegetable. Chaya blooms frequently and both male and female flowers are borne together at the end of long flower stems. Both kinds of flowers are small, less than 10 mm long. The white male flowers are much more abundant. In the fall trials at Gainesville, FL, seed pods about 1-inch wide and the size of walnuts were produced.

Culture

Chaya is cold sensitive and should be started at the beginning of a warm season. Thick woody stem cuttings about 6 to 12 inches long are used, but they root slowly. Cuttings can be established in the soil if the soil is well drained. Early growth is slow, but after the first year the plants may be pruned and leaves may be harvested, resulting in rapid new growth. Up to 60% or more of the leaves may be removed at harvest, with enough left for healthy new growth. Since most gardeners need only a few leaves at a time, one plant harvested on a continuous basis is adequate.

Use

The use of gloves during harvesting is suggested to protect the hands from spines. Younger leaves and a bit of the stems are cut and used much like spinach. Large leaves are cut into manageable pieces before cooking. Leaves are immersed and simmered for 20 minutes and then served with oil or butter.

Chaya is a good source of protein, vitamins, calcium, and iron. However, raw Chaya leaves are highly poisonous. They contain a high content of hydrocyanic acid. In this respect Chaya is similar to cassava. With Chaya, 1 minute of boiling destroys most of the acid.

Chaya (*Cnidoscolus chayamansa*) is nicknamed tree spinach but that's kind of like calling iceberg lettuce spinach. Chaya contains more than twice as much protein, calcium, Vitamin C, iron, fiber and carotenoids as spinach, according to a USDA report published through Purdue University.

It's also much easier to grow. It's a dietary staple on the semi-arid Yucatan Peninsula but also thrives in Florida's hot, rainy summers. Some people grow both hog Chaya, which has larger leaves, and the more decorative species with smaller, deeply serrated leaves and pretty white flowers that attract butterflies. Like many tropical plants (including spinach to a lesser degree), Chaya contains hydrocyanic glucosides in its leaves. Cooking the leaves inactivates the toxic compound.

In colder climates they grow well in a sunny window, although you'll want to put it outside once temperatures are consistently above freezing. They've come back from the ground with temperatures as low as the mid-20s but they're among the first plants to lose their leaves when it gets near 30 degrees.

- Chaya is one of the most care free and drought tolerant vegetables in the world.
- Chaya plants grow very quickly and easily, and one can be assured of a decent harvest since they are virtually insect-proof, and quite flood and drought tolerant.
- Chaya is frost sensitive the plant will usually resprout from the base after a freeze or woody cuttings can be taken in (before frost) and replanted in the spring.
- They comprise part of the staple diet and are the main dietary source of leafy vegetable for the indigenous people of the Yucatan peninsula of Mexico and Kekchi people of Alta Verapaz in Guatemala.
- Growth of the plant is rapid and edible leaves and shoots could be produced within a short period (8 to 10 weeks). Propagation by cutting is easy and the

woody stem sections readily root. Few pests and diseases are known to be of any significance in the cultivation of Chaya plants.
- Information on the anti-diabetic effect of Chaya can be found at the Purdue University website.
- To propagate, all you do is cut a piece of the thick, waxy stems, let it sit for a day or so until the sap dries out, then stick it where you want a new Chaya plant. They don't root super quickly, but they always root... then grow like crazy.
- Chaya will grow in full sun to part shade. It's leggier in the shade and much less productive so I recommend full sun.
- Chaya produces greens like crazy. It's considered to be one of the most productive leaf crops in cultivation.

One or two large plants, once established, should provide the majority of dark green, leafy vegetables needed for an average family. A hedge could help feed a small neighborhood. Here's a nutritional comparison, supplied by the Mexican National Institute of Nutrition, and distributed by DIF.

Percentages are based on minimum daily requirements.

%	Chaya	Alfalfa	Spinach

Protein	8.25	3.66	2.00
Crude fiber	1.94	3.12	2.07
Carbohydrates	7.23	4.84	0.19
Calcium	421.00	12.00	49.00
Phosphorus	63.00	15.00	30.00
Iron	11.61	5.30	5.70
Vitamin A	8.52	0.74	2.48
Vitamin B1	0.23	0.13	0.03
Ascorbic Acid	0.35	0.14	0.10
	274.00	130.00	17.50

I grow kale, collards, turnips, beets and lettuce through the winter... but Chaya gets us through the summer and early fall. For a liter of tea, use 3-5 medium size leaves with whatever blend you favor. I like two bags of black tea with two bags of mint and the *Chaya* leaves, "cooked" in a glass bottle in the sun for a couple of hours and then refrigerated.

Chaya traditionally has been recommended for a number of ailments including diabetes, obesity, kidney stones, hemorrhoids, acne, and eye problems (Diaz-Bolio 1975). Chaya shoots and leaves have been taken as a laxative, diuretic, circulation stimulant, to improve digestion, to stimulate lactation, and to harden the fingernails (Rowe 1994). Like most food plants such as lima beans, cassava, and many leafy vegetables, the leaves contain hydrocyanic glycosides, a toxic compound easily destroyed by cooking. **Even though some people tend to eat raw Chaya leaves, it is unwise to do so.**

A nutritional analysis shows that *Chaya* is richer in iron than spinach, and a powerful source of potassium and calcium. Its leaves are edible cooked. In fact, it's an outstanding green generally twice as nutritious as spinach, Chinese cabbage or amaranth. The leaves are very high in protein, calcium, iron, carotene, and vitamins A, B and C. In fact, Chaya can have 10 times as much vitamin C as the orange. There is no doubt about its nutrition, there is a bit of an issue, however, with how many types of Chaya there are. Whether there is one species of Chaya with several scientific names or several different species of Chaya is a bit of a debate. The botanical name is *Cnidoscolus chayamansa*.

Start harvesting as soon as you see a couple of new leaves sprouted. Cutting encourages new growth, and the branches are pretty in flower arrangements.

A study as late as 1999 states that researchers recognized two species, *Cnidoscolus chayamansa* and *Cnidoscolus aconitifolius*. At the time the *C. chayamansa* had maple-like leaves (now called the chayamansa variety) and the *C. aconitifolius* had more indented five-lobed leaves (now called the Estrella variety.) Those two botanical names are still used, with some authorities saying they are two different species, and some— the latest view since 2002 — saying they are the same plant, just different varieties. You will also see *Cnidoscolus aconitifolius ssp. aconitifolius*, and *Cnidoscolus aconitifolius ssp. chayamansa*, and the reverse combinations.

As for varieties, some have stinging hairs like their American cousins, some don't. So not only can you have multiple confusing names you can have edible Chaya with stinging hairs and without, and different shaped leaves. Often this is whether the variety is in the wild (Chaya brava) or under cultivation (Chaya mansa.) Regardless, all should be boiled or fried though there are some reports that some of the varieties can be eaten raw. I would be careful about that since cooking drives off hydrogen cyanide. You need to cook them ten to 20 minutes though some say five minutes will do. (The resulting broth is also often consumed because the hydrogen cyanide has been driven off and the water is full of Vitamin C leached from the leaves. The raw leaves can also be used to wrap food for cooking.

Drying the leaves also reduces the hydrogen cyanide significantly. Blending will do the same IF the blended leaves are allowed to sit for several hours. The amount of hydrogen cyanide differs from variety to variety and may account for reports of some variety leaves being eaten raw. Researchers say they have found no reports of acute or chronic effects attributed to the consumption of fresh or cooked Chaya leaves. Still, it is better to err on the safe side.

Recent scientific studies confirmed what Belizean natural healers and Maya shaman have known for centuries – eating a small amount of Chaya after or as part of a meal will lower blood glucose levels.

While edibility is not an issue, finding Chaya may be. It's native to Central America and endemic to the Yucatan Peninsula. The USDA maps show it naturalized only in Puerto Rico and Hawaii. It does grow in Florida and South Texas but is ill- suited to freezes though it does grow back from the root. One local specimen in downtown Orlando has been there at least 20 years, surviving several light freezes.

The cooked leaves maintain a dense texture similar to collards. **Also cooking should not be done on an aluminum container as a toxic reaction can occur with some varieties. It is best cooked in a clay or glass container.**

It's also incredibly easy to grow and an attractive addition to the garden with its maple-like leaves and tidy growth pattern. It limits itself to about six feet in height. Plant a row close together and you'll soon have a hedge. The plants tend to be open toward the bottom, so you can create a border with low- and medium-growing herbs.

Chaya plants grow well in containers, but the roots can quickly grow through drain holes into the soil if a saucer, pie tin, or other barrier is not provided. Potted Chaya plants can be brought inside during the winter months in colder climates, and will generally survive well if placed near a window for light. They also do exceedingly well in greenhouses.

The Chaya plant can grow into a five to six meter shrub, but its weak branches are easily broken by the wind. It is therefore recommended to cut the plant to maintain a height of less than two meters.

This is common practice in home gardens, and is probably the reason that the maximum height of cultivated Chaya is often cited as 1.5 meters. Despite the need to keep the plants relatively small, Chaya actively produces large amounts of leaf material.

According to Ross Ibarra and Molina Cruz, the four main cultivated varieties of Chaya are „Estrella," Picuda," „Chayamansa" and „Redonda."

Local people differentiate between „Chaya pica" (with spines or stinging hairs) and Chaya mansa" (spineless). The authors commented," Surprisingly, when this difference is recognized, Chaya pica is unanimously thought to be better tasting than its unarmed counterpart." The stinging hairs on Chaya pica are very irritating during harvest, but disappear when leaves are cooked. Wear gloves or put your hand in a sock to harvest the leaves of a stinging plant.

Ashitaba
- Ashitaba is hardy in U.S. Department of Agriculture plant hardiness zones 7 to 9. Ashitaba is a maritime plant growing best where summers are warm, wet and humid, but with cool to cold winters, and will do well in full sun. Ashitaba is also very frost tolerant.
- It is rich in anti-aging properties that helps maintain smooth, young skin
- Germination occurs 15 days after sowing. Seedlings are slow-growing and will require about 60 days to transplant. Once past the seedling stage, the plant is fast growing. The plants prefer rich, deep, ever moist, well-drained soil and full sun to part shade. Water every other day. If you are in Arizona, give shade. If you are in Coastal Maine, give sun.

- The plants are slow growing at first but once they attain the size of your hand, more or less, they grow very quickly. Mature size is about 4 feet wide and flowering to about 5 feet tall.

- Ashitaba is one of the few vegetable sources of vitamin B-12 not derived from animal or sea plants Ashitaba is unique among the Angelicas due to its tasty edibility and the presence of substantial levels of B12, a vitamin normally not found in terrestrial plants. Most plants are devoid of vitamin B12, which is normally only obtainable through meat, fish and eggs. However, Ashitaba is a good source of this nutrient, making it an ideal supplement for strict vegetarians and vegans, who omit these foods from their diets and are at risk of suffering from a deficiency. A shortage of B12 can cause serious cognitive and nervous system problems, in addition to increasing the risk of cardiovascular disease and pernicious anemia.
- The only herb with yellow sap called chalcone. **Chalcones**, organic compounds called flavonoids, found in Ashitaba confer **potent antioxidant activity** exceeding that of red wine, green tea, or soy.

A Japanese angelica, ashitaba (Angelica keiskei) is called "tomorrow's leaf" for its ability to replace harvested foliage rapidly. It is called "tomorrow's leaf" because when harvesting one leaf from the plant, you can expect to see a new one "tomorrow." Harvesting a leaf at the break of day results often in a new sprout growing over night, being visible the following morning. The plant is incredibly vigorous and its name reflects this!

Ashitaba usually doesn't bloom until the second year of growth, but once they flower and set seed, they're done. Some will produce side shoots that can be divided to make new plants. Head them to prevent flowering if you want to keep them perennial, but don't count on a harvest the first year. Snip off their flower umbels before the buds open if you want those plants to be perennial rather than biennial.

Active ingredient – Chalcones
Unique to Ashitaba is a class of flavonoid compounds called chalcones. Research has shown that they are potent antioxidants, protecting cells from free radical damage, which is associated with accelerating the aging process and with many degenerative diseases, including cancer. They also suppress the excessive secretion of gastric juice in the stomach, which is often caused by stress and can lead to stomach ulcers. In addition they help strengthen the immune system, regulate blood pressure and cholesterol, and exhibit anti-viral and anti-bacterial activities. Ashitaba. Chalcones are rarely found anywhere in the natural world! Research has shown that the unique healing properties of Ashitaba are at least partly due to these unique compounds.

Natural organic germanium, in Ashitaba, is known to promote production of Interferon which is a defensive material produced by our body to prevent viruses and bacterias from penetrating into our cells. Germanium is valuable in the purification of blood by keeping away harmful hydrogen ions in the blood, creating an alkaline PH, increasing oxygen, and by activating blood cell replacements.

Research published in *Nutraceuticals World*, Sept 2002, astonishingly showed that **Ashitaba** <u>outperformed all other herbs</u> including green tea that were tested for their antioxidant potential based on the ORAC guide (Oxygen Radical Absorbance Capacity).

On the Japanese island of Hachijo, residents have **Ashitaba** as part of their diet, and typically have some of the **longest life spans on earth**. The plant has been an integral part of the diet on this island for hundreds of years, and is the only known plant to contain a substances called **chalcones,** discovered when scientists began to analyze the diet and environment in order to determine the reasons for the health and longevity observed.

Chalconoids are present in the unique milky, yellow coloured sap, an identifying property of Ashitaba. The leaves, stems and roots can be consumed as a vegetable or salad ingredient and a tea can be made from the leaves. The recommended dosage for medicinal purposes is one teaspoon of ashitaba powder taken in the morning and evening in a small amount of juice, followed by a glass of water. Ashitaba has a sweet herb like taste and has no known contraindications.

- **Promote blood cleansing & circulation**
- **Reduce blood pressure**
- **Regulate cholesterol level**
- **Regulate blood sugar level**
- **Reduce joint & muscular pain**
- **Enhance liver & kidney function**
- **Support digestive & G.I. health**
- **Anti-viral & anti-bacterial actions**
- **Suppress cell growth abnormalities**
- **Inhibit general inflammation**
- **Strengthen the immune system**
- **Relieve smooth muscle spasms in the arteries & bronchial tubes**

- **Enhance smooth bowel movements**
- **Remove toxic wastes from body**
- **Improve visual acuity**
- **Peri-menopausal relief**
- **Smoother skin texture**
- **Aid natural sleep cycles**

Many mistaken this Ashitaba with others in the Angelica family. The true Ashitaba (scientific name: *Angelica keiskei koidzumi*) as you can see in the photo -- the potent/medicinal variety has the yellow sap in the stem when it is more mature. I cut the largest stem of mine to show you in the photo. The base of a fully mature Ashitaba is the size of your wrist!

Ashitaba is historically referred to locally by the residents of the island as the "longevity herb", and is one of natures most dynamic nutritional food sources, and has a vast spectrum of other beneficial properties which augment a number of systems in the body, especially the immune system and the circulatory system.

Instructions

- 1

Dry your Ashitaba plants to make tea and capsules. Pull the entire plant from the soil or take clippings and allow the plant to continue growing. Hold the Ashitaba upside down and tie the stems together with any kind of string. Use a foot of string or more so you can hang the bunch up to dry. Hang the Ashitaba upside down on a nail or hook away from the sunlight. The time it takes to dry is dependent on humidity conditions. One week or less is usually sufficient

- 2

Use the stems and leaves of your dried Ashitaba plant to make a tea. Break up the Ashitaba into pieces suitable for tea. Put the dry leaves and stems in a plastic bag suitable for food, place a thin dish towel over the bag and roll a rolling pin back and forth about 10 times. You want the consistency to be like loose green tea, not a powder but pieces that are small enough that you can easily measure them with a scoop. You may need to cut the stems with a scissors.

Measure out approximately one teaspoon and put it into eight to 12 ounces of freshly boiled water. Allow the Ashitaba to steep for three minutes or more. You can eat the Ashtitaba or make the tea using a tea ball.

Use your Ashitaba plants as a healthy ingredient in soups. Add one fresh Ashitaba leaf or shoot for every two cups of soup. Remove the leaves from the plant by pinching them with your fingernails or using scissors. Wash the leaves thoroughly in cold water and then dry them by laying them out on a towel for about five minutes. Using a knife or scissors, dice the leaves into small pieces. Stir the Ashitaba leaves into the soup at the end of the cooking process so they do not impart a bitter taste to your dish. Another idea is to add them as garnish before the soup goes to the table.

- 4

If your Ashitaba plant is small, you can harvest the leaves individually rather than clipping an entire stalk. To harvest your Ashitaba plant leaf by leaf, choose mature leaves from the base of the stem or shoot. The mature leaves contain more of the active ingredients than the new shoots.

Ashitaba leaves may be added into fruit juices Use 2 to 4 fresh leaves, wash thoroughly with salt water (if available), rinse with clean water, cut in small pieces, then add to your fruit juice. Drink a glass of it once or two times a day.

In traditional medicine, the plant is seen to be a strengthening tonic. The Izu Islands used to be a place of exile, criminals and social outcasts relegated to these desolate islands as a form of punishment. The exiles were forced to withstand poor diets and hard labor. They foraged for food gathering their sustenance from the rock and sand. Surprisingly, historic records indicate that despite harsh circumstances, the exiles were healthy and lived long lives. Tradition attributes this unlikely healthfulness to the continual consumption of Ashitaba.

Immune System Tonic

Ashitaba was also seen as a powerful medicine against infectious disease. Before vaccination was introduced, whenever smallpox raged, Ashitaba was brought to the mainland to cure those infected and prevent infection in those still well. This tradition of using Ashitaba to stop smallpox from spreading started with the Izu islanders, but was well accepted in mainland Japan long ago.

Skin Tonic -Wound Healing Age

When you break the stems and roots of Ashitaba, a sticky yellow juice gushes out. In fact, this is one of the unusual characteristics of the plant. The juice which so readily flows from the plant is used topically to treat a host of skin conditions. The juice of the plant is applied to boils, cysts, and pustules to speed healing. It is used to clear athletes foot fungal infections. It is applied to repel insects and to speed healing and prevent infection in insect bites. Indeed, applying the juice of the plant is said to cure most skin conditions and to prevent infection in wounds. It is used both in chronic and acute skin complaints.

Ashwagandha (*Withania somnifera*) is an herb commonly used in ayurveda (the traditional medicine of India). Although it's not botanically related to ginseng, ashwagandha is often called "Indian ginseng" due to its supposed rejuvenating effects. Ashwagandha means 'Smell of Horse,' which refers to the fresh root's distinct horsey smell, and the traditional belief that ingesting the herb will confer the strength and virility of a horse.

Ashwagandha may also increase the potency of barbiturates (a class of drugs that depresses the central nervous system).

Ashwagandha is an Adaptogen. It is supplemented primarily for its ability to prevent anxiety. Ashwagandha's anti-anxiety effect is even synergistic with alcohol. It also shows promise for relieving insomnia and stress-induced depression.

Ashwagandha is regarded as an adaptogen (a type of herb said to strengthen your resistance to stress while enhancing your energy). Often used to boost the immune system after an illness, ashwagandha is also included in formulations that aim to treat these conditions:
The berries can be used as a substitute for rennet in cheese making

Evidence of Ashwagandha's Anti-Arthritic Activity

Research indicates that ashwagandha is a powerful anti-inflammatory. In fact, in animal studies ashwagandha has been found to be more potent than hydrocortisone, reducing swelling and degenerative bone changes more than the steroid.[24] In a clinical trial involving 77 RA patients who were given 3 grams of ashwagandha orally three times a day with milk, over 75% experienced moderate to good improvement of symptoms. When combined with frankincense, turmeric, and a zinc complex, ashwagandha helped to significantly reduced pain and disability for patients with osteoarthritis compared to the untreated control group in a randomized clinical trial.

Type 2 Diabetes

Ashwagandha may help normalize high blood sugar and improve insulin sensitivity, according to preliminary, animal-based research published in 2008

Cancer

In a 2003 study, tests on human tumor cell lines revealed that ashwagandha may slow the growth of lung, breast, and colon cancer cells.

Published in 2007, another study on human cells shows that ashwagandha may inhibit tumor growth without harming normal cells.

http://www.ashwagandha.com/references - ref34

Anxiety

In an animal-based study published in 2000, researchers found that ashwagandha had an anti-anxiety effect similar to that of lorazepam (a medication used to treat anxiety disorders). The herb also appeared to ease depression

Osteoarthritis

For a 2008 study, scientists tested ashwagandha's effects on human cartilage and found that the herb may help protect against inflammation and cartilage damage associated with osteoarthritis.

Ashwagandha in particular is known for its ability to calm, and some research indicates this herb can be used to promote sleep. In Texas, researchers noted the similarities in the sleep-inducing properties of ashwagandha and the calming effects of the well-known amino acid GABA. Likewise, ashwagandha has also been shown to ease anxiety or restlessness, as well as to reduce the symptoms of drug withdrawal. Its ability to stabilize moods and encourage adrenal recovery is highly valued by many herbalists.

But the <u>benefits</u> of ashwagandha extend far beyond mood. In India it is also used to help older patients with mental agility, cognitive ability, and memory. It is also known for its ability to fight off cold and cough symptoms. Preliminary studies give researchers reason to feel that ashwagandha also has the potential ability to decrease cancer cells without adversely affecting healthy cells.

Ashwagandha is also considered by many to be an anti-aging supplement, and it traditionally was known for its ability to provide nourishment to bones and muscles. Studies have also shown that the orange berries from the ashwagandha can be used topically to aid carbuncles, skin ulcers, and tumors. Further research looks to determine its effectiveness as a treatment for bone cancer, diabetes, bipolar disorder, constipation, impotency, rheumatism, nerve problems, memory loss, arthritis, and many other physical ailments. Its effectiveness is thought to be similar to the herb ginseng used by the Chinese.

Medical researchers have been studying Ashwagandha for years with great interest and have completed more than 200 studies on the healing benefits of this botanical. Some key examples of the healing effects of Ashwagandha are:

- Protects the immune system
- Helps combat the effects of stress
- Improves learning, memory, and reaction time
- Reduces anxiety and depression without causing drowsiness
- Helps reduce brain-cell degeneration
- Stabilizes blood sugar
- Helps lower cholesterol
- Offers anti-inflammatory benefits
- Contains anti-malarial properties

1) Osteoarthritis

For a 2008 study, scientists tested ashwagandha's effects on human cartilage and found that the herb may help protect against inflammation and cartilage damage associated with osteoarthritis.

2) Anxiety

In an animal-based study published in 2000, researchers found that ashwagandha had an anti-anxiety effect similar to that of lorazepam (a medication used to treat anxiety disorders). The herb also appeared to ease depression.

3) Type 2 Diabetes

Ashwagandha may help normalize high blood sugar and improve insulin sensitivity, according to preliminary, animal-based research published in 2008.

4) Cancer

In a 2003 study, tests on human tumor cell lines revealed that ashwagandha may slow the growth of lung, breast, and colon cancer cells.

5) Anti-Oxident: Ashwagandha is used as an anti-oxidant, as studies have shown that it can eliminate free radicals from your immune system. Free radicals are the agents that cause the breakdown of your body's tissue, alternatively known as aging.

6).Provide energy: Studies show that supplementing with ashwagandha can provide the energy needed to get through long workouts while also allowing for maximum recovery and cell re-growth.

Published in 2007, another study on human cells shows that ashwagandha may inhibit tumor growth without harming normal cells.

Uses for Ashwagandha

Ashwagandha

Use this ancient and powerful healing herb to counter the stresses of modern life. After a hard day, a cup of *ashwagandha* tea can help relaxation and promote sleep.

Ashwagandha roots are long fleshy tubers that are cream colored. If you can grow tomatoes then you can probably grow ashwagandha as they need a similar climate, Ashwagandha is regarded as an adaptogen (a type of herb said to strengthen your resistance to stress while enhancing your energy). Often used to boost the immune system after an illness, ashwagandha is also included in formulations that aim to treat these conditions:

Ashwagandha is known to affect certain bodily processes which aids in improving bodily functions. Its general action in the body is to increase the oxygen capacity within the red blood cells. Adequate oxygen supply in the body results to better brain and organ functioning.

Ashwagandha may be helpful for reducing the effects of stress, including chronic psychological stress. Since ashwagandha has sedative effects, it could help ease anxiety and stress -- in fact, human studies have indicated as much. *Ashwagandha* is a member of the nightshade family, which also includes tomatoes—but, unlike the tomato, the quarter-inch, orange-red fruits of this herb are not the focus of its beneficial properties. The mature plant's thick, gray taproot, which reaches 1 to 2 feet into the soil, contains compounds that act as a sedative, reduce anxiety, and induce relaxation.

GROWING NOTES
Native to India, Ashwagandha bushes will grow to heights of 3 feet or more and produce light green flowers from midsummer onwards which will develop into orange or deep red berries by fall.

Ashwagandha prefers full sun and fairly dry conditions, and has low to moderate water needs.

A*shwagandha*, a tender perennial, can be grown as an annual in climates with cold winters. Plants started from seeds will yield reasonably sized roots during one growing season. Ten to 12 weeks prior to the spring frost-free date, sow seeds in flats or individual pots indoors, much as you would tomato or eggplant seeds. Seeds germinate within 2 weeks.

When the weather is warm and there is no chance of frost, transplant the seedlings to a spot outdoors in full sun or partial shade. In fall or early winter, when the berries ripen and leaves begin to dry, pull the plant up and cut off and dry the root, washing it carefully before placing it in a dry and dark place indoors. When dry, the root can be chopped and used to brew tea or made into an extract.

Ashwagandha can be direct sown outdoors following the last frost, approximately 3/8" below the surface of the soil and kept evenly moist. Otherwise, you can sow indoors in early spring to give your starts additional time to develop before going outside. Sow seeds slightly closer to the surface (~1/4") if using flats or other small containers indoors.

☐ As an insecticide, it is useful for killing lice infesting the body. An ointment prepared by boiling the leaves is useful for bed sores and wounds.

☐ The fresh leaf juice is also applied for anthrax pustules.

In Africa the root is given as a sedative to children and to soothe teething pains.

The berries can be used as a substitute for rennet in cheesemaking.[

To grow ashwagandha, you will need a seed tray as they require care and careful attention while they germinate. Here is how to grow them:

1. Place one to two Ashwagandha seeds into each compartment of the seed tray and press them gently into the surface of the soil. Do not cover the seeds with soil.
2. Place the seed tray in a location that receives bright sunlight and maintains a constant temperature.
3. Mist the top of the soil daily with water from a spray bottle and do not allow the top of the soil to dry out. If you prefer, you can fill a tub with 2 inches of water and set the seed tray into it to water it from the bottom.
4. Wait until the Ashwagandha seeds germinate in approximately two weeks.
5. Continue watering and observing the plants until they reach 3 to 4 inches high and transplant them outdoors to a location with full sun and sandy soil.
6. While transplanting, be sure to leave 2 to 3 feet between each plant. Water well and keep the plants moist until they begin to show strong signs of growth. After that time, keep your ashwagandha fairly dry.
7. The plant is ready to harvest in about 6 months.

As always, avoid using any herb if you are pregnant, breast-feeding, or trying to conceive without the specific advice of a healthcare professional.

10

Commercial Applications

There are many ways to enhance your gardens bounty as you have seen but there are technologically advanced commercial versions for sale that one might consider.

Commercial Applications

Moving in my two Garden Towers.

I did a major upgrade to Prepper Shack this year and added these unique growing systems. http://www.gardentowerproject.com/ use coupon code Prepper1 if you decide to purchase one please.
http://linkis.com/gardentowerproject.com/Q2nFw

I have one for growing my own botanical plant pharmacy and the other for growing vegetables. The only reason I am using a collapsible hand

Commercial Applications

truck that I keep in my van is because I assembled this one and it needed to be inside the fences protection from deer before I filled it with dirt. That's not a deer fence but they don't jump it very often.

Soon to be my turnstile salad bars. A "Garden Tower Project" planted with various kinds of lettuce, chard etc.

These come packaged in a box and can be moved around or thrown in a trunk for a bug out if you had the room. When I was talking to the companies owner I inquired about what kind of a discount or how much did he want for a pallet of those things and remembered that picture I had from the Texas Garden Towers Face book page. That's where this books cover idea came

Commercial Applications

about. Wow what if I had unlimited resources or was setting up a prepper community and had me a trailer of these things I said jokingly to myself and then got to studying just what I could do with mine. I guess that will be in my next book because I have just got fired up this season with my two units and want to finish a whole season with them.. So far they are very well made and a excellent resource for me to expand my gardens capabilities. I found that they would be a great way to start seeds for transplants in a bug out situation, a means of creating fertilizer and a host of other things I will expound upon one day.

A driveway gate project made of castle block with a worm tower added. Ashitaba on right. Having "Tomorrows Leaf and" Heal All growing at the

Commercial Applications

entrance to my property just somehow seemed to me a fitting and proper thing.

No Keyhole entrance here, instead a few blocks to stand on to throw compost into the pipe.

Commercial Applications

Goji, Golden Scalloped Squash and Asparagus lettuce, Beet Berry

Commercial Applications

Goji Bushes, Bok Choy and Ashitaba

My Tomato Machine I made out of watering trough with the fantastic Texas Tomato cages that are the only ones that are going to be strong enough for those Italian tree tomatoes I am growing this year to tower over. Trip L Crop is a Great choice for such a setup also. I am

Commercial Applications

hoping for 2 bushels large luscious tomatoes off these two plants this year.

I added worm towers to my raised beds with mixed results because of the dirt under the garden soil is solid clay. Some of the beds I had to abandon this practice for awhile because they would retain water, adding a cap to the pipe should be a solution though. That is curly Kale growing.

Commercial Applications

Anxiously watching and growing this year's crop after a 2 week rain deluge and thinking about the next book.

Commercial Applications

Ah Tree Tomato is taking off and loves my Bug Out style fertilizer.

Commercial Applications

Added, Malabar spinach transplants to the four posts on my Tree Tomato trellis. This variety will vine up and the plant likes very hot summers so its permaculture for my area. Good growing my friends, thank you for your patronage.

THE END

Industrial Strength Tomato Cages.
Texas Tomato Cages
Tomatocage.com

COUPON CODE PREPPER1

Introducing the Terracotta Garden Tower

Coupon Code Prepper1

KEYHOLEFARM.COM

Keyhole garden kits and accessories.

SilverFire

Coupon Code Prepper1

King's Mountain Seeds
The Orginal Disaster Plaster
"Just Throw And Grow!"

My Readers Might Also Enjoy:

**THE RURAL RANGER A SUBURBAN AND URBAN SURVIVAL MANUAL & FIELD GUIDE
OF TRAPS AND SNARES FOR FOOD AND SURVIVAL**

By Ron Foster

The Modern Day Survival Primer for Solving Modern Day Survival Problems! This book will teach you the techniques to not just survive, but to use ingenuity and household items to solve your problems scientifically with a bit of primitive know how thrown in. A complete and detailed section utilizing explicit drawings and easy to understand photographs covers thoroughly the topic of survival trapping using Modern Snares, Deadfalls, Conibear Traps, and Primitive Snares. This book is dedicated for long term survival in the country or the suburbs to insure you survive and thrive! Build a solar oven or pasteurize water its all in here! Catch your dinner, then cook it or preserve it, too! Food procurement is the name of the game along with purified water in a survival or disaster situation. Are you ready?

Check Out The Original Prepper Trilogy

Preppers Road March

A solar storm has just hit the world causing an EMP event. An emergency manager visiting Atlanta GA must find his way back home after this electromagnetic pulse has stranded him away from his vehicle and his beloved "bug out bag". With 180 miles to go to his destination, David must let his street smarts and survival skills kick in as food and water becomes scarce and societal breakdown proceeds at an unrelenting pace. An interesting and often funny cast of characters from the Deep South helps the displaced Prepper on his way, as he shares his knowledge of how to make do with common items in order to live another day. Ultimately, he acquires an old tractor and heads for home on a car-littered interstate. This is book one of the Prepper Trilogy.

BUG OUT! Preppers on the move!
Book two of the Prepper trilogy finds the disaster planner and emergency manager Dave faced with the choice of bugging out with his cohort of friends and family as he watches the societal collapse and demise of civilization around him after an electromagnetic pulse (EMP) solar storm has taken out the grid. A post apocalyptic fiction series that takes you through the trials and tribulations of

survival after the predicted NASA 2012 solar super storm unravels the lives and lifestyles of a group of modern day survivalists. The preppers decide on a lake front bug out with bags in hand as well as a unique group of operating vehicles from a bobcat loader to a lawn tractor. Will they survive? Could you? Let us find out, and join the party down the desolate dystopian landscape of a new beginning in a world without lights or technology.

The Light in The Lake

Book three of the Prepper Trilogy finds our band of refugees from a solar storm safely moved into a several lake cabins and trying to work on their short term and long term survival. The lake is a beautiful place for a survival retreat, but is it safe with roving groups of lake residents all looking for what meager food resources remain after a EMP event has shut down society as we know it. Can society be recreated and restarted here, or will starvation and anarchy take over? Can a simple light in the lake be the solution to survival and the reconstruction of society, or is it merely a symbol of what has been and might be yet again?

Lightning Source UK Ltd.
Milton Keynes UK
UKHW02f2153061117
312303UK00005B/649/P